RESTLESS REDHEAD

D1426052

Joan Killilea with two young Thai friends.

Restless Redhead

by
Virginia Anderson

Director of Pioneer Girls, USA

LONDON
OVERSEAS MISSIONARY FELLOWSHIP

Copyright © 1968 by Pioneer Girls
of Wheaton, Illinois, USA
as *A Restless Redhead and God*

This edition	..	*June 1970*
Reprinted	..	*March 1971*

ISBN 85363 079 8

Published by Overseas Missionary Fellowship
Newington Green, London, N16 9QD

Printed in Great Britain by Billing & Sons Limited
Guildford and London

"Thou hast made us for Thyself,
and our hearts are restless till they
find their rest in Thee."

St. Augustine

Contents

Monkey Hill

A STURDY little redhead lay flat on her stomach on the living-room floor, heels kicking in the air, absorbed in the picture section of the Sunday paper. Big blue eyes in a round face peered intently through thick glasses. She was seven now, and could even read a few of the captions to the pictures. As she turned the pages, one picture caught her imagination and she stared at it, fascinated. Then she looked up at her father with a question.

"Daddy! Look at the children in this picture. They're so thin and their clothes are just old rags. What's wrong with them? Are they sick?"

Thomas Killilea glanced down at his daughter. "Those are Chinese children, Joan. There's a war going on in their country and they don't have enough food or clothing. They're starving to death." Tears began to form in Joan's eyes.

"But why doesn't some one help them? I wish I could." She paused, then announced firmly, "Daddy, do you know what? When I grow up, I'm going to be a missionary nun and go to help children like that."

Tom Killilea smiled. "Perhaps you will, Joanie, perhaps you will," he replied.

Joan jumped up and ran out to play with her sisters and brother on Monkey Hill. But often the newspaper picture haunted her in quiet moments. And she would determine anew that some day she would help such children.

Monkey Hill was not on any map. Its official name was Highland Place, a cul-de-sac on a hill just outside Boston

in the USA. It had been called Monkey Hill because of
all the lively, noisy children who lived and played there.
At one end of the street was the grammar school, at the
other end were the woods. The Killilea home lay between
the two – a white three-storey wood-built house big enough
to accommodate the five Killilea children and their parents.
The third floor was an attic – one huge room and the
perfect place to play on a rainy day.

Joan was the middle one of the five Killileas. Joan's
mother was a Canadian who had been a night club dancer
before her marriage. June was the child of a previous
marriage, then came John, Joan, Mona and Pat, whose
father was one of seven children born to Irish immigrants
from County Cork. He had followed his father into the
laundry business and stayed in it. Joan took after her Irish
father. Whenever one of the Irish relatives observed that
"Joan looks like a Killilea", her father used to reply,
"Sure an' she has her share of the ol' Irish wit, too. She's
just full of ideas for games or jokes or stories to act out."

Joan took the opportunity to improve her dramatic
talents when a neighbour began taking elocution lessons.
Joan saved her pennies and persuaded the girl to teach her
what she had learned for the modest fee of ten cents a
lesson. Joan then entertained her Monkey Hill audience
with recitations. Her favourite was "A Song for a
Tomboy" – a perfect description of herself.

That boys outnumbered girls on Monkey Hill did not
bother Joan at all. She could climb a tree as high, throw
a ball as far, or run as fast as the best of them. She greatly
admired her brother John and loved to accompany him
on his early morning paper rounds, even on the coldest
winter days.

One day there was great excitement on Monkey Hill.
The O'Connells, a neighbouring family, had bought a
goat. "Quick!" shouted Joan. "Come and see the
O'Connell's goat! They're hitching him to a cart!" The

rest of the day the patient goat was busy pulling cartloads of children up and down the hill.

Life on Monkey Hill was full of carefree fun and adventure for seven-year-old Joan – except for one thing. Her father, whom she dearly loved, was ill and in and out of the Chelsea Naval Hospital. One day Joan came home from school to find her father already home from the laundry lying on the couch. "Your dad isn't feeling well," said her mother. "I've called the doctor and he's on his way."

"It's nothing, Joan," her father assured her. A little medicine from the doctor will fix me up fine."

But it was not as simple as that. Once again Tom Killilea had to return to hospital. The weeks dragged into months and Joan began to wonder if her father would ever get well again. And when she felt sad at the thought, Joan loved to take long walks in the friendly woods, following the winding path that led past tall oaks and pines and huge granite boulders to the quiet swamp pond. She remembered the fairy tales she had heard about Irish leprechauns, and in the silence of the woods could easily imagine that a leprechaun was watching her as she hunted frogs or practised skipping stones on the still pond.

The woods offered new delights and adventures with each turn of the season. In the autumn she shuffled through the dry, crackly leaves piling up in the hollows. In the winter she skated on the pond and joined in the snowball battles. When the snow and ice melted she used to search for the first wild flowers and signs of life in the pond. In the summer, when the blackberries ripened, Joan loved to pick the sweet juicy fruit. Summer was also the best time for games of hide-and-seek or cops-and-robbers – there were so many good hiding places in the thick green foliage. But always in the back of her mind was the thought of her father, lying ill in hospital.

At last, Tom Killilea came home from hospital. That afternoon, Joan, now eight years old, could hardly wait to get home from school to see her father. When the closing bell rang, Joan burst out of school, ran up the street and dashed into the house, letting the door slam behind her.

"Is Daddy home yet?" she shouted.

"Shhh! Not so much noise, Joan dear," her mother answered. "Yes, Daddy's home, but he's not quite better yet so you must be very quiet and let him have lots of rest and sleep."

Joan tiptoed up the stairs, but then burst open the door and shouted, "Hi, Daddy!"

She stopped short when she saw her father. His face was chalky white and haggard. She hardly knew him.

"Hullo, Joan," he said with a weak smile.

Joan walked slowly over to the bed and kissed her father. "Daddy, are you awfully sick?"

When the other children arrived, Tom Killilea spoke to them quietly.

"Children, I have something to tell you. I won't be with you much longer. When I'm gone I want you all to obey your mother and be good children."

Stunned, the children stood in silence.

"No, it's not true, Daddy," said Joan tearfully, "You'll get better. You *must* get better!"

But it was not to be. Tom Killilea grew worse and one day Joan's uncle put his arms around the smaller children and said to them all, "I'm sorry to have to tell you this, children. Your daddy has died!"

Late that night, Joan's numbness dissolved into great racking sobs, and she beat her fists into her wet pillow. "Why did it have to be my daddy?"

After that life was different in the Killilea house on Monkey Hill. There was still fun and adventures outdoors. But with their dad gone, the secure, stable family life the children had known was disrupted. Mrs. Killilea had taken work as a waitress, and the irregular hours at the restaurant meant that the children were often left alone to care for themselves. The loss of her husband and the care of five children proved too great a burden for Joan's mother and she began to turn for solace to various men friends. The younger girls enjoyed the "uncles" who brought them sweets and played with them. But Joan loyal to the memory of her father, resented their visits.

When the situation did not improve, the Killilea relatives agreed to take custody of the children. One night an aunt and uncle came to fetch them. Joan's mother was not at home. Questions tumbled through Joan's mind as she climbed into the car. "Why are we going away? Where's my mother? Why isn't she here to say goodbye? Is this really just a holiday or are we leaving Monkey Hill for good?"

Lonely Years

JOAN did not have to wait long for answers to her questions. In the next few days the five Killilea children were divided up among various relatives. Joan went to live with her Aunt Claire and Uncle John on the second and third floors of a large old two-family house in Hyde Park, another Boston suburb. For a time, Joan's brother, John, also lived there.

The aunt and uncle already had their hands full with three boys and later a girl of their own. Now with John and Joan added to the household there was never a dull moment. Four years of living and playing with these boys did little to make a lady of tomboy Joan. When bad weather prevented outdoor play, she and the boys turned to improvised "indoor sports", such as sliding on pillows down the long hall upstairs. Afterwards they carefully turned the pillow-cases inside out in the hope of hiding the tell-tale dirt from Aunt Claire.

On one occasion the four boys locked Joan in her third-floor bedroom. Undaunted, she climbed out of a window on to a tree branch. Unfortunately her clothing got caught in a branch and there she hung in a most undignified position while the mocking boys sang "Pennies from Heaven". Sometimes when there were visitors the girls slept together in the big double bed in Joan's room. One night after they were safely tucked in bed and the aunts and uncles were deep in conversation downstairs, there was a gentle tap on Joan's door. "Come in," Joan called softly. The door opened quietly and cousin Page tiptoed in.

"Are you ready?" he whispered.

Joan jumped out of bed, pulled on a coat and rolled up her pyjama legs. Then she felt under her pillow for some carefully saved pennies.

"O.K." she whispered. "Let's go!"

She and Page crawled out of the third-floor window on to the tree branch and slid cautiously down to the roof of the porch. From there it was easy to slide the rest of the way down. They hurried off to a local shop and soon return-ed with a big bag of sweets which they shared with the other children. Suddenly there was the sound of footsteps on the stairs. Quickly the boys disappeared under the bed and the girls slipped back under the bed-clothes. When the door opened, a light from the hall fell across a peaceful scene with three girls sleeping soundly.

Joan had boundless energy as well as a strong will and a stubborn streak so that sometimes she was difficult to handle. Deep within, she was lonely and insecure, but managed to hide these feelings from the outside world. Trying hard to impress her boy cousins and older brother she certainly did not want to be thought a sissy.

It soon became obvious to Joan that the separation of the family was to be permanent. Mona and Pat had been formally adopted, How Joan envied her two younger sisters, who now had a real mother and father again and a lovely home of their own, with many pretty clothes and other nice things! With her freckles, glasses and "awful red hair" Joan felt that nobody wanted her.

At fourteen Joan went to live with another aunt and uncle for the three-and-a-half years of high school attendance. But she was unhappy – quiet and unimpressive. Because of her poor marks she had to switch from the pre-college to the commercial course, and even then did only average work. Her abilities lay in other areas – sports, creative crafts and dramatics. She played basketball well, but was not picked for the school team because of her poor class-work. Wanting badly to play for the team Joan made a special effort to get better marks, but in vain. Her report was as bad as ever.

In her disappointment Joan began to daydream about the future, as she often did when she was depressed. "When I finish high school, I'll get a good job and earn lots of money. Then I'll buy all the things I want – pretty clothes, a car, a home of my own. I'll take riding lessons, and learn to play tennis and golf. I'll be popular and have boy friends." Pleasant pictures drifted across the screen of Joan's imagination. She saw herself in a long, filmy green evening gown (green was her favourite colour) stepping out of a sleek sports car and smiling up at a handsome young man as they entered an exclusive country club. Then she imagined herself on a tennis court, racket in hand, wearing a smart white tennis outfit, with the same handsome man for a partner. In the next scene she was riding on a graceful white horse, galloping across a wide green field, followed, of course, by another horse with the same young man – or maybe another one this time! Why confine herself to just one admirer?

With such thoughts occupying her mind, Joan felt happier. She was passing her church and decided to go in. The two things which comforted Joan when she was discouraged were her dreams about the future and her religion. She loved to walk through the cool, dimly lit, quiet building. Ever since early childhood, Joan had felt a holy awe whenever she stood at the altar and looked up at the crucifix. Now she gazed long at the figure of Christ, hanging there on the cross with nails in His hands and feet and a crown of thorns on His head. How sad He looked – how infinitely sorrowful! What a terrible death He had suffered! This was how she always thought of Jesus – hanging on the cross, dying. Her heart went out in pity to Him. But she dared not approach Him directly. So she moved on, past the statues of various saints to kneel finally before the statue of the Virgin Mary, whom she dearly loved.

"O Mother of God, you're so beautiful, so pure. You're my true Mother. O Queen of Heaven, your mantle, like the blue of the sky, be over me and protect me. Keep me pure. I want to be your loyal daughter. O pray for me to your Son Jesus."

During her final year of high school Joan moved back to Hyde Park, Massachusetts, where a little attic room was to be her home for the next few years. On June 7, 1945, the day before her eighteenth birthday, Joan came to the end of her school-days. Her uncle offered to pay for further schooling, but she refused. She had had enough of school. Now she could get a job and earn her own money. At last she was free to make her own plans and shape her life as she wanted.

Dead-End Streets

"Look, Aunt Julia. How do you like my new outfit?" asked Joan as she pranced into her aunt's room and whirled around gracefully, her long red hair swinging loosely against her shoulders.

The aunt put down the newspaper, pulled her reading glasses down her nose, and peered at Joan. She was a short, heavy Irish woman with a pleasant, round face and snow-white hair. Her bright blue eyes revealed a lively, energetic nature despite her advanced years.

"Sure an' don't tell me yer spent yer whole pay packet in one day again," she scolded. "Ye really ought to be openin' a savin's account, Joan."

"Does this colour suit me?" interrupted Joan, ignoring her aunt's advice.

" 'Tis indeed a pretty suit," admitted Aunt Julia grudgingly, "but those shoes aren't very practical – such high heels! Why, ye've no support at all. Sure an' ye can't do much walkin' in them."

"Now, don't ye be worryin' bout me, Aunt Julia. Sure I can walk fine," Joan imitated her aunt's brogue as she gave her a squeeze. "And what's more, I didn't spend a cent of me pay packet. I charged the whole shebang!"

"Och, the saints preserve us. That's still worse," cried Aunt Julia with a disapproving frown.

Joan glanced at her watch. "Oh, oh! The rehearsal for our minstrel show begins in fifteen minutes. I've got to hurry." Joan ran from the room, leaving her aunt shaking her white head in despair as she turned back to her reading.

"Life is exciting," thought Joan as she changed her clothes. "It's fun being a long-distance operator at the telephone company, especially on pay day. Of course Aunt Julia's right. My pay cheques don't last long. But after all, I needed a whole new wardrobe – plus jewellery,

17

make-up and hair style. It sure has made a difference in my appearance, though." Joan admired her reflection in the mirror. "My old friends in high school wouldn't recognize me now."

It was gratifying to have young men take notice of her looks. Joan had begun to date – had even had a proposal from one young man already. But she wasn't ready to settle down yet; besides, she didn't think he was the right one for her.

Joan glanced around the room quickly to be sure everything was in order, for she hated an untidy room and always kept everything neatly in place. "At least that's one thing Aunt Julia doesn't have to scold me for," she thought. Although small, with a slanting ceiling, the attic room was bright and cosy. There was only room for a double bed, a dresser and an easy chair. "When I can afford it, I'll move out of this place and find a place of my own – a place I can fix up the way I want," she thought as she switched off the light and hurried off to the rehearsal.

The minstrel show was produced by the St. Angela's Roman Catholic Club, of which Joan was social chairman and later vice-president. The show turned out to be a huge success. Three evening performances and a children's matinée were given before a total of over 2,000 spectators. Joan's flair for dramatics made her a natural choice as producer.

There were other boarders in the house besides Joan. Each morning Joan's aunt arose bright and early to bake her own bread. She used to prepare the dough and let it rise while she hurried off to Mass. Later, the smell of baking bread and fresh coffee was an incentive to the rest of the household to get up in time for breakfast.

When Joan was nineteen, her sister Mona moved into the little attic room with Joan and the two sisters got to know each other again. Mona was finishing high school in Hyde Park. Tiny Mona, with her blonde hair and green eyes, was quite a contrast to Joan, who was tall and athletic. Joan introduced Mona to her favourite activity of horse riding. Passionately fond of horses, Joan had become an excellent rider. Mona loved to watch her sister on Big Red, the horse she loved best at the stable, for he was the same colour as Joan's hair, and a powerful horse; few could handle him, but Joan had no trouble. Joan's room was decorated with pictures and figurines of horses and she looked for a horse design in whatever she bought – jewellery, stationery, or anything else.

Mona and Joan sometimes did things together with their brother, John, who was also back in the Boston area, having returned from the war in Europe with a bronze star for risking his life to rescue a wounded comrade. The girls were justifiably proud of John who was handsome, stable and dependable, much like their father. They loved to listen to his fine tenor voice, and soon became good friends with his fiancée, Norma.

One day, in a supermarket, an unfamiliar woman approached Joan and asked, "Are you Joan Killilea?"

Surprised, Joan answered, "Yes, how did you know?"

"Because I'm your mother."

Joan had not seen her mother, now remarried, since childhood days. And they met as strangers. Joan's feelings were mixed, but the relationship she would like to have cultivated was not to be. Later she was to understand something of the emotional anguish her mother must have experienced in letting the family be scattered, and she bore no bitterness towards her.

When John and Norma married, Joan spent many happy hours in their home. They were both enthusiastic about antique collecting and interior decorating. Joan, too, was clever and creative as well as handy with hammer and saw, and she loved to help Norma paint and re-do her rooms and furniture. Often the two went antique hunting or scouring the beaches for driftwood which Joan made into many attractive lampstands as gifts for her friends.

When Norma had her first baby, Robbie, Joan was thrilled to have a nephew and to become his godmother. Joan always had loved small children, even as a teenager.

But despite a good job, money to spend, friends and hobbies, Joan became increasingly restless. She left the telephone company and tried a variety of jobs; clerk at a dry cleaners, maid and governess for a wealthy family, cashier in a supermarket. She also changed her "digs" frequently. Once she even moved back to Monkey Hill where she lived with a family who had known her as a child and treated her as their own daughter.

Among Joan's new enthusiasms was an old second-hand car in which she spent many carefree hours. She also learned to play tennis and golf. Joan had now become a thorough-going extrovert. No longer the quiet, unobtrusive girl of high school days, she was everywhere the life of the party. With her irrepressible Irish humour she kept her friends entertained for hours and boasted, "When the funny stories are passed around the night club tables, I can top 'em every time!"

Joan was enjoying life to the full – sports, hobbies, parties, friends, dates. What more could she ask for? This was really living – or was it? Sometimes Joan wondered. Why was it that whenever she paused in her whirl of activity she felt the same lonely restlessness that she had known as a teenager? Then she had comforted herself with dreams of the future; now those dreams had been fulfilled, but still the emptiness remained.

"What is the matter with me?" she thought on one of those rare evenings she spent at home alone. "I have all the things I used to long for – money to spend as I please, a wardrobe full of clothes, a car, popularity, fun, boy friends. Why am I still dissatisfied? Is this all there is to life? Surely God has created me for some purpose, but what is it? Where can I find the answer?"

Perhaps the answer was to be found in marriage. Joan fell in love with a young contractor, and they became engaged. They spent many happy hours planning the house they would live in. With her fiancé's skill in carpentry and Joan's talent at interior decorating, theirs was to be a veritable dream house. Surely there she would find fulfilment and happiness as a wife and mother. Joan was ecstatically happy – except for one thing. Her fiancé was a Protestant and showed no inclination to turn Roman Catholic. But Joan was optimistic. Surely he'll change his mind. But time went by and wedding plans progressed, and still her fiancé had not changed his religion. The issue could not be postponed. Once more she pleaded with him. "Won't you at least attend an instruction class in the Roman Catholic religion – so you can find out what Roman Catholicism really is?"

"For the last time, Joanie, I'm not interested. You don't want me to change to your religion if I don't believe in it, do you?"

"No," Joan admitted. "You mustn't do that just to please me. You must be convinced yourself that the Roman Catholic Church is the one true Church – and of course it is. Why can't you see it?"

"I love you very much, Joanie. But if you want me as your husband you'll have to take me as I am, a Protestant, or not at all. It's up to you to decide."

That night in her room Joan faced the most bitter struggle she had ever known. She had to chose between the man she loved and the Church which she dearly cherished. For hours she debated with herself. "What shall I do? All these years I've yearned for a home of my own – for someone to love, someone who would love and care for me. Now I've found that one, I just can't give him up – I won't! I want desperately to marry him. And yet, how can I disobey my Church? How can I disappoint Mother Mary?"

Joan was deeply devoted to Mary and to marry a non-Roman Catholic would be to betray Mary. Through the night the battle raged in Joan's heart. As dawn approached, she finally slipped exhausted into a troubled sleep. The next day, her painful decision made, she broke off her engagement. Loyalty to her Church had won the day.

Heartbroken, Joan became more restless than ever. She tried to join the armed services, but each time she failed to pass the doctor because of poor eyesight. Joan even joked about this. She told friends, "The doctor said, 'Remove your glasses and walk toward the chart until you can read the first line'. I took them off and started walking until I bumped right into the chart!" And she ran smack into a wall to demonstrate.

Joan next considered becoming a nun. "I've done everything I can possibly do in my Church except enter a convent. I go to novena, mass, confession, communion, stations of the cross, and yet I come away feeling dissatisfied. Maybe the answer is to take the last step and become a nun. Surely then I'll find contentment."

Impulsive Joan might have packed her bags and gone off right away to a convent, but relatives discouraged her. "Joan, this is no time to make such an important decision, just after a broken engagement, before the wounds have healed. You're trying to run away from yourself, and that's not the right motive for becoming a nun. Give yourself plenty of time to think it over before you take such a step."

Joan knew they were right and she took the advice. But oh, the aching longing of her heart – how was it to be stilled?

And so Joan, now twenty-four, continued her search – a search that seemed to lead only down dead-end streets.

The F.M. Leprechaun

ROBERTA SCHOFIELD entered the huge old building of the Factory Mutual Insurance Company in downtown Boston, and headed toward the lift. Slim and attractive with short dark blonde hair, she walked with an assurance that she did not feel.

Her friend, Ruth Redden, greeted her with a wide smile. "Hi, Berta. Well, today's the big day – your first at Factory Mutual." Ruth was twenty-four, a year older than Roberta. Her tailored suit and shoulder-length brown hair gave her a trim appearance. The two girls entered the lift.

Roberta spoke. "Isn't it a funny world? I never dreamed when I studied fashion designing that I'd end up as a draughtsman in an insurance company. What a let-down!"

"I felt the same way when I started working here. But I think of it as only temporary. I hope to do some art-work on the side and maybe some day earn a living at it. But meanwhile it's good that art school graduates are welcome in the draughting field." Ruth and Roberta had both graduated from Massachusetts College of Art the previous spring. Ruth's special subject had been commercial art.

The draughting department was on the sixth floor. Here copies of factory plans were made so that insurance costs could be estimated. Ruth introduced Roberta to Mrs. Edith Preston, the supervisor, who then led Roberta to a draughting board and gave her some instructions. Mrs. Preston's quiet, gentle manner put Roberta at ease at once and she soon became engrossed in her new work.

Roberta had only been working for about fifteen minutes when a sudden commotion made her look up. A redheaded girl raced in and jumped on to the stool next to her.

"Whew! Late again!" the girl gasped breathlessly. "I

only hope the big boss didn't see me. He bawled me out just last week for being late so often."

"Your old Ford break down again, Joan?" called a male voice from a nearby desk.

"Not this time. I had to drive round the block three times before I found an empty parking meter. You know, Jim, I don't use those car parks any more. I reckon I can save about fifty cents a day using meters. That's $2.50 a week."

"And you're going to run down to put five cents in the meter every two hours? You're crazy."

"So what?" the girl replied. "At least I'll get some fresh air and exercise."

"Since when have you become so thrifty anyhow?" called another voice. "You must have some Scottish blood mixed with the Irish in your veins!"

"Huh, the only way I get Scotch in my blood is when I drink it," retorted the redhead.

Meanwhile Roberta was observing her new neighbour. What she saw was an attractive girl with long red hair, twinkling blue eyes behind dark-rimmed glasses, and an infectious grin. She wore vivid red lipstick, a bright green dress with a white chiffon scarf at the neck and high-heeled shoes which she let drop to the floor as she curled her toes around the rung of the high stool.

Suddenly the redhead turned to Roberta. "Say, you're new here. My name's Joan Killilea. What's yours?"

"Roberta Schofield."

"Welcome to Factory Mutual, Roberta. I'm the Factory Mutual Leprechaun. Here's my card . . . " and she pointed to a card on her draughting board. Roberta read the following poem:

"I'm 'Loafer', the F.M. Leprechaun,
    Sure, 'tis the sixth floor I work on,
    With no more earthly thing to do
    Than paste on a lil' patch or two,

But if you should call me on the phone,
Don't ask for 'Loafer' . . . they call me Joan!"

Throughout that morning Roberta tried to concentrate on her work while Joan kept up a steady stream of chatter. Occasionally, Joan looked over at Roberta and teased, "Roberta, you talk too much. Are you always so noisy? Can't you be still for a while?"

Despite her chatter, Joan was a fast, efficient worker, and quick to lend a helping hand whenever Roberta had a question or problem about her new work.

During the morning Roberta looked up to see the fellow called Jim creeping up behind Joan to snatch her shoes from under the stool. Then he tied a string around them and hung them out of a window. Joan was too engrossed in telling Roberta of her escapade the previous evening to notice anything.

"You know, Berta – you don't mind if I call you Berta, do you? You can call me Joanie – anyhow, yesterday a gang of us got a wild idea. You'll never guess where we went. We just had an urge to take off for somewhere and someone said, 'Let's go to New York City and hit some of the high spots – you know, some famous night clubs.' So we did. We left right after work."

"You mean you drove down and back in one evening? Why, that's about 200 miles, isn't it?"

"Well, let's say we drove *down* in the evening. We didn't drive back till this morning, of course. In fact, I just had time to change my clothes and have a cup of coffee before coming to work."

"You had no sleep? You must be exhausted!"

"Not really. Of course, I slept a bit in the car. We took turns driving. It was worth it, though. We had a marvellous time."

Just then Mrs. Preston came in. "Joan, the boss wants you to run an errand for him."

"Be right there," said Joan, looking around for her shoes. Seeing that they had disappeared, she quickly grabbed Roberta's shoes from her feet, slipped them on and went off on her errand.

"What a nerve!" thought Roberta, "My first day at work. I hardly know her, and she takes my shoes without even asking!"

When Joan returned, there was commotion until she found and recovered her shoes. Settling down at her draught board again, she said, "Tell me about yourself, Berta. Where did you last work?"

"I graduated from art school in June and then spent the summer counselling at a girls' camp in Maine. This autumn I took a temporary job decorating at a Woolworths' shop."

"Is that right? I once had a job decorating at Woolworths. In fact I've had lots of jobs. I've only been here at F.M. about six months now. But speaking of art school," Joan chuckled and lowered her voice, "I wrote on my job application that I went to art school, too – so that I'd be sure to get a job here. I named a school in Portland, Maine, one that doesn't even exist."

Roberta was shocked. "Weren't you afraid they'd write to the school for references?"

"Oh, I knew they wouldn't bother," was Joan's flippant reply.

At noon Joan went off to have lunch with a friend, while Roberta and Ruth ate their sandwiches together.

"Who is this girl, Joan something? I can't remember her last name," said Roberta.

"Joan Killilea. It's an Irish name. Did you meet her?"

"Did I! She sat beside me all morning and talked non-stop! She seems to be quite a character."

Ruth laughed. "She is. She's the bright spot in the office – a real case! But she's great fun."

At the end of office hours, Joan cleaned her brushes,

then solemnly walked down the aisle between the rows of draughtsmen with her brush and glass of water, and sprinkled a little on each one. "I bless *you* . . . and I bless *you* – and I bless *you* . . " Everybody laughed. Obviously Joanie, the F.M. Leprechaun, was a general favourite.

A week or two later, Roberta and Ruth had just sat down to eat their lunch when Joan joined them. "Hi!" she said. "My friend doesn't work here any more so I'm going to have lunch with you both." There was a bit of a pause, then, "I hope you don't mind."

"O no," replied Ruth and Berta hastily. From then on the three lunched together daily. Often they used the lunch hour to go shopping – they especially kept a watchful eye on Filene's basement so as not to miss any special bargains.

Joan sometimes invited Ruth and Berta to go out with her, but both were very active in their local churches and had no time to spare.

"Joan seems lonely to me," said Ruth one day. "She obviously wants to be friends with us. But what can we do together? We have so little in common."

"Yes, she enjoys going to shows, night clubs and dances, and you'd think a girl like her would find us rather dull."

Far from finding Ruth and Roberta dull, Joan was indeed attracted to them. They were friendly and Joan appreciated the way they had so readily accepted her when she barged into their friendship. They were different from anyone she had ever known before. She wasn't quite sure why, but she was determined to find out.

One day Joan had a bright idea. "How would you two like to go to the big circus at the Boston Garden?"

"Sounds all right," the two agreed. "Where can we get tickets?"

"Never mind tickets. Artists can get in free to sketch the animals, and they can go right down to the front to get the best view."

"Sounds great," Roberta said, laughing.

So the three of them took pencils and sketch pads and off they went. Joan saw a tattooed man at the back entrance and asked him where artists could get in to sketch. He told them which door to try and said, "Tell them Jake says it's O.K." So they went to the door and Joan announced confidently to the guard, "Jake says we can go in here to sketch." The guard made no objections, so in they went, mingling with clowns, elephants and midgets about to go into the arena. There they sketched happily throughout the performances – Joan acting for all the world like a seasoned artist, but being careful that no one looked too closely at her sketches.

In the following months the three went about a lot together, for Ruth and Roberta shared Joan's love of adventure and were always ready for fun and new experiences. In the spring the office organized an outing to a beach south of Boston, to be followed by a banquet and a dance. Joan invited her new friends to drive down with her. They accepted, but said they would not stay for the dance, so, after the banquet, they drove down to Cape Cod. Unfortunately it was early in the season as well as late at night and they could find no motel open. Finally they slept in the car – Joan on the front seat, Roberta on the back seat, and Ruth on the floor with a blanket. The next day they explored the Cape. Joan was thrilled to find that her new friends also enjoyed browsing through antique shops and combing the beaches for driftwood. That night they drove home weary but happy.

For months Joan watched Ruth and Roberta closely. She visited their girls' club and actually occasionally went to church with them. Her two new friends seemed so happy and contented with an inner peace and strength that she herself lacked. They talked of Jesus Christ as if He were a personal Friend, not a stranger. This was all so new to Joan. "Can this be what I've been seeking all

these years?" she wondered. She had never dared to go
directly to Christ, but had always approached Him through
Mary or a saint.

When someone said to Joan, "Why do you go around
with those two all the time? They're so religious," her
reply was:

"Maybe so, but they really live their religion."

Joan asked many questions. "Why do you believe this?
Why does your church do that? Why won't you go with me
to a night club?"

Ruth and Roberta patiently answered the questions.
"Joan, when I was in high school," Ruth explained,
"Jesus Christ became a real Person to me. I realized that
He, God's Son, had died for me to save me from sin. I
asked Him to take control of my life and He became my
Saviour and Friend. It had nothing to do with joining a
church, Joan. It was getting to know a Person, Jesus
Christ. And, well, He changed my life, my ambitions,
my values, my interests. That's why I don't do some of
the things you do. An evening of drinking and dancing in
a night club just isn't my idea of fun."

"What about you, Berta? Did you have an experience
like Ruth's?" asked Joan.

"Yes, only much later. Actually I came to know Christ
through Ruth. In college she was active in the Inter-
Varsity Christian Fellowship, an organization for students.
She and others met for regular Bible study and prayer.
A friend of mine began to attend and before long she,
too, became a Christian. Both she and Ruth tried to
persuade me to come to their CU meetings. But I wasn't
interested in Bible study, though I went to church. I
was busy having a good time and didn't feel I needed any
more religion. Then Billy Graham came to Boston and
Ruth and Flora invited me to go. My curiosity got
the better of me. I went and that evening I realized that,
although I was a church member, I didn't really know

Jesus Christ. So I asked Him to come in and take over my life. And He did."

Joan was quiet for a few moments. Then she said, "Well, you have your religion and I have mine."

The friends discussed, but never argued about their beliefs. Sometimes there was good-natured banter, as when Joan complained that her boy friend, George, always invited her out on Friday nights when she could eat only fish. "Why don't you change your religion?" Ruth teased.

In the early summer of 1952 Joan rented a little cottage of her own, beside a lake in the country. She called the place "Spooky" and spent many happy hours fixing it up. Roberta and her sister Barb helped her paint the outside of the house. Joan loved to entertain at the cottage and one day she asked Ruth and Roberta and five friends of theirs for supper and the night. Sleeping bags under their arms, several of them met in the rush hour to drive out with Joan in her old Ford.

"Boy, am I a fish out of water in this crowd?" was Joan's comment during a brief stop at a friend's house.

At the lake the girls had time for a swim before a tasty spaghetti dinner. In the evening they sat on the floor by the fire and read stories from *Winnie the Pooh*. Then they sang folk songs, camp songs and hymns. The hymns were new to Joan, but she liked them as they seemed to express such joyful trust in God. Joan wished she could join in, but when they suggested having prayers she excused herself to do some work in the kitchen. Finally everyone rolled out the bedrolls on the floor in front of the fire and fell sound asleep.

Most of the guests that evening were planning to be counsellors at a camp run by an organization called "Pioneer Girls" which was to run for four weeks in August. As Joan listened to the discussions of the plans, she became more and more curious to find out what it was all about. Roberta had a load of supplies to take up to the camp on the opening week-end, and since she had no car, Joan offered to drive her up so that she could see the place about which her friends talked so much.

Joan wrote the following verses for Ruth and Roberta before they left, to express her appreciation for their friendship and, more than that, her desire to become like them:

> I can't begin to tell you
> How sad and lost I'll be
> When 146 hours from now
> You'll be bidding farewell to me.
> But I shall ask the Father up above
> To please protect the ones I love,
> Keep them always safe and sound,
> No matter with whom or where they're found.
> Watch them closely through the day
> While they're teaching Your children the right way.
> Help them to know and help them to see
> Exactly what You want them to be.
> And last of all, dear Lord, I pray,
> That You will make me as strong as they.

An Outsider Looking In

"Boy, this camp really is in the backwoods," Joan said, as she steered her ancient Ford down the long, narrow, winding dirt road leading to "Camp Cherith". She managed to miss the trees and bushes lining the road, but she could hardly avoid the ruts, bumps and loose rocks in the middle. "Guess I'd better slow down," she added when a rock thumped against the bottom of her car.

At last they came to a turning where a large sign indicated the entrance to Camp Cherith.

Joan stopped the car and got out. "I have an idea,"
she said. "Come on, Berta. Give me a hand."

Before Roberta could agree or protest, Joan had pulled
out a big sheet of paper from a box of supplies and had
started to cover all the car windows. Berta joined her and
soon there was only a tiny space on the front windscreen
to see through. Joan then crayoned in large, bold letters
"Camp Cherith – or burst!" all around the car. Tooting
the horn full blast they roared the rest of the way into
the camp.

The camp staff, busily preparing for the arrival of 120
campers the next day, stared in amazement at the strange
vehicle as it emerged from around the bend, wound down
the steep hill and jerked to a standstill in front of the
handicraft cabin. The car door opened, revealing an unfamiliar redhead still leaning on the horn. Joan Killilea
had made her "grand entrance" to Camp Cherith.

It didn't take them long to unload the supplies, and
soon the new arrivals, too, were hard at work cleaning cabins
and moving beds. The rest of the week-end Joan scurried
around with pieces of board, hammer and nails. She was
putting up shelves beside the counsellors' beds – an act
which endeared her to their hearts.

But Joan was not too busy to notice the beauty of her
surroundings. The camp was situated on a steep hill overlooking the clear blue waters of Bunganut Lake. The
dining hall and office were perched high on the hillside;
further down the hill were fifteen white cabins in a semi-
circle; behind them paths led down through a pine grove
to the lake. A small, shady beach provided an ideal place
for swimming. Joan fell in love with the place at once.
"It's even lovelier than my lake," she admitted to her
friends.

Of even more interest to Joan than the camp site were

the people and the camp programme. She decided to return. The following two week-ends Joan drove to the camp with the excuse of transporting campers; but she always stayed for the whole week-end and attended all the activities, including the evening campfires, the morning Bible study groups, and even the Sunday morning services – after returning from early Mass herself. Hearing of plans for a "Winnie the Pooh party" one week-end, Joan rented a bear costume with an authentic-looking bear head from a store in Boston. She was just in time to join the festivities, and, as usual, stole the show!

Hearing that the camp was short of kitchen help Joan offered her services.

"I hear you need help in the kitchen," she said to her friends. "I'll take the last week of August off and come to work in the kitchen. I'm no great cook, but I can peel vegetables and open cans."

Ruth and Berta reported to the director, Ginny Anderson. "What do you think of Joan working in the kitchen for a week?"

Ginny hesitated. "Well, we don't usually employ anyone even for kitchen work who is not a committed Christian."

"Yes, we know. But can't we make an exception for Joan? She seems so eager to know more about the Bible. We really think this is the reason she wants to come."

Ginny agreed.

Joan's decision to work at camp was not lightly made. When she had asked her supervisor for permission to take the week off, Joan had said, "It's a Protestant camp, and I'm not really sure it's right for a Roman Catholic to work there."

"Why don't you ask a priest about it?" Mrs. Preston suggested. This Joan did, receiving the answer that it was all right so long as she did not join in the singing or give any contributions. So Joan felt she could go to camp with a clear conscience as far as her Church was concerned.

B

It is a Camp Cherith tradition that all staff members are called by bird names, and Joan was named Chimney Swift, soon to be shortened to Swiftie. She was a great help in the kitchen and entered into as much of the camp life as her work permitted. In the evenings she attended a camp-fire, and evening prayers in Ruth's or Roberta's cabin. Joan's reaction to all that she heard was, "It's all very interesting, but it's not for me. I have my own religion."

It was not until years later that Joan revealed her real impressions of camp. "My, what a strange situation I found myself in! Everyone had a Bible, something I had hardly seen before. I shall never forget the camp-fire singing, especially from a little nine-year-old who always sat beside me and sang from the bottom of her heart, 'In my heart there rings a melody'. How my own heart would ache because there was no melody at all there; quite the opposite. I went home from camp without accepting Christ; the One who loved me and gave Himself for me. It was such a new and wonderful story; could it really be true?"

The camp officers had learned to love Joan with her friendly, fun-loving spirit and her eagerness to help, but they also sensed her restlessness. They knew she was searching for meaning and purpose in life. She was like an outsider, looking in longingly, wanting so much to know this Lord Jesus who seemed to be such a reality in the lives of the officers and many of the campers. And yet, she wasn't sure – she wasn't yet ready to put aside the teaching of her Church and come directly to Christ.

On the last night of camp Swiftie sat quietly at the camp-fire service. She looked up at the silent stars scattered across the heavens, then down at the tall trees silhouetted against the placid lake. Between the songs and testimonies she could hear the soft lapping of the lake against the shore and the occasional crackling of the friendly camp fire. How she wished there was the same peace in her heart that she found in nature around!

The little blonde camper who had taken a special liking to Swiftie was sitting beside her again. Suddenly, the girl got up to give her brief testimony, telling how she, too, had taken Jesus into her life and wanted to live for Him. As she sat down again, she turned to Swiftie and said, "Now you give yours!"

But Swiftie sat immobilized. She had no testimony to give.

Entering the Fold

> And ye shall seek me, and find me, when
> ye shall search for me with all your heart.
> (Jeremiah 29.13)

Camp was over, but Joan's contacts with the camp officers continued. Back in Boston she missed camp and her friends who had remained to help pack equipment and close the camp, so she and two other officers decided to drive down after office hours, spend the night at camp and return early next morning in time for work.

Joan's old Ford was notorious for its breakdowns and her brakes had not been working well of late. As the three approached the toll-gate on the motorway, Joan remarked, "What if my brakes won't work?" They didn't. As the car glided past the startled attendant, Joan called out cheerily, "Be right back!" When the car rolled to a stop she backed up and paid the toll. The attendant, thinking Joan was trying to be funny, was annoyed.

The rolling Maine countryside dotted with farms and woods was lovely that night in the pale light of the full moon. As they turned into the familiar track leading to camp, the trees cast eerie shadows on the narrow road before them. At the last bend Joan turned off her lights and stopped the engine so as to arrive quietly and surprise everyone. But all was silent. There was no sign of life and there were no lights in the buildings.

"Surely they can't be in bed already – shh, what's that?" Sounds of splashing and voices drifted up from the lake. "They're having an evening swim."

In the dining hall they found sleeping bags laid out on the floor by the fire. "They must all be sleeping here instead of in the cabins. Let's get into their sleeping bags and surprise them!"

The three invaders kept silent as the swimmers returned and groped in the dark for dry clothing. The flickering light from the fireplace was reinforced by soft moonlight filtering in through the windows. As three shadowy forms emerged from the sleeping bags there was an ear-splitting shriek. "Turn on the lights!" screamed someone. After a boisterous few minutes, everyone settled down for the evening.

Joan continued to attend meetings where she heard the Gospel. One week-end she went with Ruth and Roberta to a retreat sponsored by Inter-Varsity Christian Fellowship. On the very first evening Joan was deeply stirred by the speakers, and that night God began to break down the walls of resistance she had built up.

Soon a gigantic struggle was taking place within Joan's heart. She spent long hours discussing her beliefs and doubts with a friend who patiently answered her questions from the Scriptures, but it often seemed as though their discussions went in circles.

Joan's biggest obstacle in coming to Christ was her devotion to Mary. "I can't give up my faith in Mary.

Surely something terrible will happen to me if I do,"
Christ had never had much place in Joan's faith; her
devotion was to Mother Mary, to whom she prayed and
from whom she expected help.

As Joan began to read the Bible for herself, she found no
support for such exaltation of Mary. Verses like, "For
there is one God, and one mediator between God and men,
the man Christ Jesus" (1 Timothy 2.5) indicated no need
for any intermediary, be it Mary, saint or priest. The
believer may go directly to Christ. This discovery shook
Joan's firm belief in the exalted position of the Virgin. She
became confused. The long hours of discussion with Joan
began to wear on Ruth. Yet she knew this was a crucial
time. God's Spirit was speaking to her friend and she was
putting up a hard struggle. Remembering a Christian
doctor who had once been a Roman Catholic, and thinking
that he might be able to help Joan, Ruth asked her if she
would be willing to meet him. "Yes," Joan said, "if you'll
go with me to an instruction class I'm attending for
Protestants who are interested in the Roman Catholic
Church."

Ruth agreed and made an appointment with the doctor
for the same evening as the class. First Ruth went with
Joan to the class, where the priest demonstrated that the
Protestant and Roman Catholic versions of the Bible
were almost identical. After the class, when Joan went to
express her doubts to the speaker, he merely patted her
on the back, smiled and said, "Just keep going to Mass."

The later appointment with the doctor was out in a
suburb. Joan suddenly got cold feet and wanted a drink
to brace her spirits.

"Just one drop of gin," she pleaded.

Ruth was firm. "It won't help, Joanie."

Finally Joan was ready to go. The doctor she had
dreaded meeting simply told how his life had been changed
through the personal presence of Christ.

"Huh, the doctor didn't convince me of a thing," Joan complained, driving Ruth home afterwards.

The weeks went by and Joan's friends began to despair that she would ever come through to a living faith in Christ.

Finally, one night in November, Joan could resist no longer. This, in her own words, is what happened:

"The Lord got me to a place one night where I could hear the Good News again. I was invited to a meeting at which a chalk artist was to speak. But the chalk artist never came. I don't even know who it was, but God had His plan. That night the speaker said, 'I want to talk to you tonight about the One, the only One, who can ever satisfy a lonely hungry heart.' I sat there listening again to the Good News about the Lord Jesus, and that night I decided to ask Him to become my own personal Saviour. I went home with my friend, and when she knelt down to pray, so did I, and I told the Lord I wanted to be His, completely His. That night the Lord Jesus Christ became mine and I became His."

Ruth, the friend in question, was not aware of this at the time. All Joan said was, "You don't have to bother to pray for me any more." Did this mean that her prayers were answered or that there was no hope they would ever be? But gradually it became apparent that Joan had now passed the crisis and stepped over the threshold from death to life in Christ. At last she had capitulated to Jesus Christ, the Son of God.

In December Joan went with friends to hear Handel's Messiah sung in Boston. She had never heard it before and was deeply moved by the words. When the chorus sang, "All we like sheep have gone astray", she was overcome with emotion. The words and music described so graphically her own experience of long years of straying until the Good Shepherd found her. How she loved the tender description of the kind Shepherd in the solo, "He shall feed His flock".

That evening Joan saw herself as the lost sheep who, all her life, had searched and yearned and hungered. At last she had met the One who came to seek and to save the lost. She had entered the Good Shepherd's fold and was experiencing that love which alone can satisfy "the longing soul and (fill) the hungry soul with goodness" (Psalm 107.9). It was the end of a long search, but the beginning of a new life.

Toddling at His Side

As Joan began her new life with Christ she felt very much like a little child learning to walk, which she expressed in the following words written on the back of a photograph she gave to Ruth.

"It is a glorious privilege to be a Christian. The most exalted privilege any mortal man can have is to walk through life hand in hand with Christ as Saviour and Guide, or to put it more correctly, to toddle along at His side, and though always stumbling (or should I say, always falling flat on my face?) never letting go of His hand."

Joan knew that she now belonged to the family of God, but, like any young child, she had her growing pains, her ups and downs, and even times when she "fell flat on her face"; yet she never did let go of His hand.

Actually Joan grew rapidly as a Christian. She said, "I knew the night I received Christ that it didn't mean just giving the Lord Jesus first place in my life, but it meant giving Him my life completely, for Him to do with it whatever He wanted." And so she tried to discover just what it was God wanted her to do with her life. In February, 1953, Joan was baptized at a church where she remained a member for the rest of her life. There she began at once to take an active part in the life of the church, assisted Ruth with her Pioneer Girls' club, helped in the Sunday School, and became a member of the young adult group.

Romance might easily have entered Joan's life at this stage, for a young man in the group began to date her, but she had her eyes fixed on another goal. In 1953, feeling the need for Bible training, she applied to Gordon College and was accepted. In the testimony Joan submitted with her application she wrote, "I have decided that I must go to school and learn more about my new-found Friend so that I may be able to talk intelligently to my old lost friends."

But going to college meant money for tuition, room and board – and Joan had none. Up to this time she had never saved a cent; instead she had accumulated debts. So first of all she sold her beloved old Ford, though she did not get much for it. She found a rather unusual part-time job in the home of an elderly lady in the Back Bay area. It was a typical stately old Bostonian house, built of red brick and covered with ivy. Joan had to look after the house, its tenants and the dog while the owner went away for several months. She even had the use of the lady's car. Her large basement room served as bedroom, kitchen and living room.

She soon realized that she was poorly prepared for college studies after being out of high school for almost eight years and never having really learned to study. Coming into the Bible courses at Gordon in the middle of the year, with no background Bible knowledge, was too much for her. She scarcely knew who Paul was, and even the best known Old Testament stories were unfamiliar. So she became very discouraged.

Then, too, some of the Christians Joan met did not measure up to Ruth and Roberta, and after her long search before finding peace in Christ she had little patience with shallow Christians who did not take their faith seriously.

During one of her blue periods Ruth sent her the following letter:

"To my 'fightin' Irish' Friend –

"Don't give up the battle. Remember, you're on the winning side and you're not fighting alone. He goes before you and you're just toddling along behind. So you stumbled again – He only permits it so you'll know your weakness and so you'll let Him be your strength. So you feel alone – He wants you to take your eyes off earthly friends and to show you how little they amount to compared to Him. Who else is so understanding? 'What a privilege to carry *everything* to God in prayer.'

" 'The Lord God is a sun and shield: the Lord will give grace and glory; no good thing will he withhold from them that walk uprightly' (from Psalms). Don't take your eyes off Him, and don't set your hope on anything but His promises, Joanie. When this passes over, He'll mean all the more to you. Wish I could help, but you don't need human friends. But I love you."

Another time Ruth, Roberta and her sister Barbara were having coffee with Joan, who was particularly despondent that evening.

"Cheer up," said Roberta. "Things can't be that bad."

"They're worse! With the marks I'm getting, I may as well give up college." With these words she got up abruptly and walked out, leaving the three sitting there all the more convinced to pray Joan through.

Once when Joan was praying with a friend, she heard

her speaking so freely and simply to God as if conversing with Someone intimate.

"How can you talk to God like that?" Joan asked wistfully.

"Because He's my Father," was the reply. Joan never forgot that answer and often closed her letters with the words "Because He's our Father".

Joan began to appreciate the spontaneity of Protestant services, but often missed a sense of reverence. Of the Roman Catholic Church she said, "In their churches they have it all around them – the Gospel story. Yet so few of them see it." It was not simply a new Church she had found but a Person, the living Christ Himself. And she longed that her old Roman Catholic friends, too, might see beyond the doctrines and forms of worship to the Person of Christ.

When summer came, Joan was invited back to two camps in Maine and in the Pocono Mountains of Pennsylvania, this time first as a counsellor and then to work in the kitchen. Joan was delighted to have the opportunity but had misgivings as to her ability to help spiritually or love adequately. But God answered prayer and gave her such rewarding experiences that she returned for the next three summers. Joan wrote:

"I am so thankful for the opportunities I have had to tell others of my new-found Friend. I've received many answers to prayer. I know that there is nothing that can compare with the joy and strength which come with introducing others to the Saviour."

At camp Joan's fun-loving personality was a great asset and she was in her element when it came to performing stunts. She and a younger counsellor, Kitty, made a good team with their quick wits and excellence at impromptu skits.

One of the stunts they laid on at Pocono camp almost turned into a tragedy. The campers were gathered outside for a water show. Suddenly "Swiftie" appeared in outlandish clothing and high boots, wearing daubs of poster paint make-up, and carrying an open umbrella. Kitty was running after her, squirting her with water from a fire extinguisher. As Swiftie yelled "I don't want to get wet," she "accidently" fell into the pool and got soaked. However, she had not realized how deep the water was. As she could not swim, her waterlogged boots dragged her down. Quickly realizing the situation, Kitty jumped in, helped Joan out of the boots, and the two emerged with the wet poster paint streaking down their faces and clothing. The campers roared with laughter, not realizing the danger that had been averted.

Swiftie contributed much to the morale of the camp and sometimes made pizza for the tired camp staff to enjoy after campers were asleep.

But Joan had a serious side to her. She heard some graduates talking about Columbia Bible College, where many of the students were older and preparing for the mission field. Joan, now twenty-six, decided that this was the place for her.

But there was still the money problem. What Joan was earning at camp was little more than pocket money. She later testified:

"I remember one morning at camp having my quiet time by the lake. The Lord Jesus spoke to me through Luke 12.22–24, 'And he said unto his disciples, Therefore I say unto you, Take no thought for your life, what ye shall eat; neither for the body, what ye shall put on. . . . Consider the ravens: for they neither sow nor reap; which neither have storehouse nor barn; and God feedeth them: how much more are ye better than the fowls?'

"And then the Lord said, 'Swiftie, I died for you . . . . You're much more valuable to Me than the birds and I take care of them. Won't you trust Me to take care of you?'"

And so, trusting Him, Swiftie sent her application in to the Bible college. She was advised to wait until January to enter, and this gave her the autumn months in which to earn some of the needed money. In September she returned from camp to work in a school for the mentally retarded.

"My work consists of caring for fifty-six girls, ages five to fourteen. Their mentality averages around five years old. I have them in my care completely for eight hours a day, thus giving me many opportunities to tell them stories about our Lord. It's a very new and strange type of story for them and it is very difficult to know just how much they grasp, but I'm thankful for Isaiah 55.11 telling us that His Word shall not return void. I have no Christian fellowship here, but have found that being in such an environment you have to walk hand in hand with the Lord or else it would be a most depressing place to be in. He has taught me so many lessons here and I have used for my verse Matthew 25.40, 'And the King shall answer and say unto them, Verily I say unto you, Inasmuch as ye have done it unto one of the least of these my brethren, ye have done it unto me.' "

Those who observed Joan in her work were impressed. She was patient and kind with the children, sometimes buying them little surprises and planning parties for them, and the children were very fond of her. At Christmas the school presented a programme to the public. A friend of Joan's who attended said:

"It was very moving to me to observe Joan with the retarded children and to watch them as they repeated the Christmas message which she had so lovingly taught them."

During the autumn months Joan spent many of her days off with Roberta's parents. The Schofields treated her like one of their own daughters; they always had the welcome mat out and prepared good home-made food for her. Mrs. Schofield and Joan shared a love for antique shops and Joan helped the Schofields redecorate their house, outside and inside. During this time, too, Ruth, her spiritual adviser, was married and went to live at some distance. So the close relationship between Joan and Ruth came to an end, and, though difficult for Joan, she saw God's hand in it removing the "prop" which she had so sorely needed in her first steps along the Christian way.

Finally the day came for Joan to say goodbye and board the bus to the next stopping place on her life's journey – Columbia, South Carolina. The toddling stage had now ended, and she was taking big strides in her Christian life. But much training was still needed before she would be strong enough for the work for which God was preparing her.

Whirlwind in the Dorm

JOAN enjoyed her first trip into the deep South. "It was a pretty ride through the southern states, especially for an old Yankee. I just love the state of Virginia with its rolling hills and old plantations. The ride through the Blue Ridge Mountains was really terrific. As I looked at nature, I wondered what makes it so beautiful; I came to the conclusion that it's because it offers no resistance to God. We, too, can only let the beauty of Jesus be seen in us when we come to this same place in our lives."

There was no fanfare to announce Joan's arrival at Columbia Bible College as there had been at Maine Camp, Cherith. Nevertheless, her arrival made a lasting impression. The administrative offices were then housed in a large, stately white, Spanish-style building with tall arches at the entrance, which had once been a hotel. There were offices on the first floor and on the other three floors where the women's dormitories were also located.

Miss Elva Brownlee was sitting in her office at the head of the stairs on the second floor when she heard a great commotion. Hurrying out of her office to see what it was all about, she saw in the hall below a strange redhead flanked by suitcases, jovially introducing herself to some other students in a booming voice which echoed up the staircase. Joan Killilea had arrived.

Years later the staff and students at Columbia still retained vivid memories of Joan; friendly, fun-loving, boisterous, often running through the halls and bounding up the stairs two at a time, bubbling over with an infectious joy, cocky and sure, invigorating, neat and original in decorating her room, unused to discipline. The dean summed it up in the words, "She was like a whirlwind in the dorm."

Joan's boisterous personality stuck out a mile in the quiet, dignified halls of the southern Bible college, where rules were strict and women students were expected to behave like ladies. It became a familiar sight to see Joan scrubbing down the stairs, a penalty for being noisy during study time or after quiet hours at night. Joan was not intentionally breaking rules, but had simply never learned to subdue her naturally exuberant temperament. Subsequently, in Thailand, Joan was thankful for the training in self-control, because the gentle Thai people find boisterous, loud behaviour offensive.

Joan had a strong will and was not accustomed to submitting to authority. If convinced she was right, she would sometimes disregard the rules. For example, on Christian service assignments, the students were instructed to counsel only those of their own sex. But Joan once admitted in a student prayer meeting that she had counselled a man, and added, "*The Lord* gave me permission".

"She was like a wild horse needing breaking in," said

the dean. "Although she had the ability to be a general, she needed to learn to be a private first. She had zeal without knowledge, but her heart was aflame for God." The dean and Joan always kept on good terms, despite the fact that Joan needed occasional discipline. Joan deeply admired and respected the dean and appreciated her wise advice. Miss Petty, in turn, recognized Joan's potential, realizing that her stubbornness and tenacity, when properly tempered, would be valuable qualities in missionary work, where persistence and perseverance are sorely needed in times of difficulty and discouragement.

Once when Joan returned quietly to her room after an interview with the dean, her room-mate asked, "Hi Joan, where have you been?"

"I've been to see Miss Petty. You know, that woman is a woman of God. She knows just how to deal with me. . . . " (Pause) " . . . They say sheep and lambs are awfully dumb animals. I think I fit that description. I'm no good at work and I'm always doing something wrong and getting into trouble. But I *am* His lamb and He is *my* Shepherd and I will always follow Him."

"Right now you look like a little lamb who has felt the Shepherd's rod," was the comment.

For Christian work Joan was assigned to a Pioneer Girls' group, of which there were only four in the whole state, so she was highly delighted. "I have twenty little 'grim pills' [nickname for Pilgrims] and had the joy of leading one to the Lord this week. Have them on Tuesday nights and would appreciate your prayers."

Writing to a friend, she said, "It would thrill you to watch the students at mail time when they open their letters and receive cheques from people they don't even know, sometimes on the very day the payment of fees is due. I stood there amazed to see the Lord doing such mighty things for these girls because they obeyed and trusted Him. But Killilea said, 'Oh, that couldn't happen to

me'. This attitude bothered Killilea, so finally she made
up her mind to stop doubting what the Lord could do for
her. That night I put the whole situation before Him and
told Him that I would trust Him completely for my
financial need. The next morning Killilea went down to
collect her mail and, lo and behold, there was a cheque
for $10. Well, you can well imagine how I felt. But that's
just half the story–you see, I had given this money to
someone for room and board where I stayed on my way
down to school over a month ago. I want you to note the
Lord's perfect timing. This person could very well have
sent the money back to me right away; but no, the Lord just
waited until I submitted to Him. It made me think of
Joshua crossing the Jordan. The Lord didn't divide the
water until Joshua stepped into it, trusting the Lord to do the
rest. And so it was with me. I just had to take that one step."

The letter went on:

"Rules and regulations are a little rough for an old
stager. . . . Am having to adjust to a room-mate. This old
gal [meaning herself] has been on her own for too long
and just enjoys being alone. After praying much about it,
I came across this in a little book of daily readings: 'We
have not to develop a spooky life of our own apart from
the ruggedness of human life as it is.' This just fitted
me – even the word 'spooky' was so perfect, because that
was the name of my cottage! Just give me time! I'm learning that there is someone else in the world besides Killilea.

"Here at college they have prayer groups for all countries
and religions except Roman Catholics, so I asked the
dean why they forgot that religion. Her answer was that
no one had ever started one. Well, now if you come to
CBC on a Wednesday night between 5.30 and 6, you
can pray for Roman Catholics, and how well each of you
know how to do that. (Thanks!)

"Thought you would get a kick out of this – last night
somebody put a bird's nest in my bed and of course I

didn't find it until about half an hour after lights were out. What a feeling! I wonder who will get it tonight? Maybe my room-mate! She's as quiet as can be; you never saw two such complete opposites in your life; Oh well –

"Please forgive me for making carbon copies, but I'm learning the value of time along with many other things. In fact I'm learning lots in the heart but very little in the head (Gulp)."

This, then, was the whirlwind who had landed at Columbia Bible College, eager for all that God had for her as she entered this new phase of her life.

Lessons in Trusting

THE small amount of money Joan had when she entered Columbia was soon spent. She took a part-time job during the term and each summer she received some remuneration for her work at camp. But for most of her needs at Columbia she had nowhere else to turn except to God. In February, 1955, she wrote to a friend:

"I marvel at His love for each of us. With the end of term comes the little matter of finances for the next term. In order to register you must have your fees! Well, registration day was on Monday; the week before I had told the dean my situation. The Lord had already sent me $40 of the $126 needed. I told her I was sure He would supply the rest. She told me to keep on praying and to let her know how things turned out.

"Six days went by and no more money came in, but there were two mail deliveries on registration day. There was a great financial need throughout the whole student body and the Student Loan Association was exhausted. Many eager students were at the mail box, including Swiftie, with an eager eye on Box 183. Sure enough, an envelope. When I opened it, there was $20. This certainly was a thrill, but I still needed about $70, and the next delivery brought no letter for me.

"In to the dean I pranced – I didn't know whether to take my suitcase with me or not. She greeted me with, 'Well, Joan, I've been waiting for you all day. I received a cheque for you this morning for $109.' Honestly, it's a good thing I learned at camp not to ask why, because so many students had to go home for lack of funds. All that keeps going through my mind is, 'Unto whomsoever much is given, of him shall be much required.'

"It would be fun to write a story, making believe I was Swiftie's mail box. It brings so many blessings. Many times just an envelope with nothing written on it, but in it money, or an envelope with ten three-cent stamps, or one with even a pair of stockings in it. Last week a card with a subscription to *His* magazine, with no name signed to it. Then there are always those dear little slips of paper that come to tell you there's a package for you. The Lord uses such precious ways of showing me His love. The most wonderful way, of course, is when He tells me Himself."

Swiftie especially loved to tell Pioneer Girls groups the following account of God's goodness to her:

"One Christmas I wanted a new suit. I was going home and I asked the Lord for money. I prayed for a week – no money. Prayed for two weeks – no money. Three weeks – no money. And so I talked to the Lord Jesus some more. 'Lord, I guess maybe I don't need a new suit, because You've told me You'll give me what I need. You've never failed me, so guess I don't need it. And I went off to class.

"But when I got back to my room, there on my bed was a box, all wrapped up with brown paper and string. And on the outside of it, it said, "Pioneer Girl Swiftie,

Columbia College, Columbia, South Carolina'. I tore off
the string and then the paper. There was no return address
on the outside, so I didn't know who sent it. I looked
inside for a card but there was none. Then I dug a little
deeper, and you know what was in it? A new suit. And you
know, it was my favourite colour – green. Oh, what a lovely
Lord Jesus we have, who is interested in every detail of
our lives! And of course, you know that the suit fitted
me perfectly because the Lord Jesus, who knows every
thought we have and knows what's way down in our
hearts, knows of course what size Swiftie wore. Oh, God's
a wonderful heavenly Father."

An entry in Joan's diary shows that she did not take
for granted the numerous gifts from others, many
anonymous.

"So let me live that when I see
The ones who've sacrificed for me,
I can in truth and honour say:
I have not thrown your trust away."
– *Douglas Parsons*

"Lord Jesus, I thank Thee for Thy loving care and
that once again Thou hast supplied my need. Thank you,
Lord, for Thy dear children. Wilt Thou bless the giver
of the $135? May he be willing to give of himself as well
as his substance. O Lord Jesus, wilt Thou make me a
faithful and obedient child this term?"

Although money matters were at times a problem to
Joan and a challenge to her faith, an even greater difficulty
was the matter of studies. Joan had been accepted at
Columbia only on probation, because of a deficiency in
English and her poor grades at Gordon. She was an
earnest student, eager to get all she could from her classes,
but study was hard. Her real talents lay in working with
people, in organization, and in using her hands. She was

creative and original, whether planning a programme, acting out a skit, doing a craft project, or decorating a room. But she was not a scholar.

While studying for her first-term exams Joan wrote to her friends asking for prayer.

"It's a little rough for an old fellah to get the cobwebs removed, but just as long as I pass everything and get an A with Him, that's all that matters."

An entry in her diary from her last year at CBC shows how much she had depended on God to help her in her studies.

"How I thank Thee, Lord Jesus, for all that Thou didst allow me to accomplish today in my studies! Wilt Thou enable me to finish in order that I may take my finals? Made five book reports. Wrote three papers. Only Thou dost know what a miracle that is!"

A few days later she wrote, "Exams were enjoyable today. Thank you, Jesus, for prayer partners. Wilt Thou bless them as they intercede for others?"

The Lord did not fail Joan. Although her marks were below average, she passed all her courses.

The testimony which Joan gave at CBC just before leaving for the mission field made a lasting impression on many there.

"When God called me to be a missionary, I said, 'Lord, I want to go, but I don't know what you're going to do with me. I'm not a teacher, I'm not a nurse. You know I don't have any talent. What can I do for You?' He said, 'Joanie, I'm not looking for clever boys and girls or men and women, I just want clean boys and girls and men and women.' And then one morning in my quiet time, the Lord said, 'And now Joan, what doth the Lord . . . require of thee, but to fear the Lord thy God, to walk in all His ways, and to love him, and to serve the Lord thy God with all thy heart and with all thy soul?' (Deuteronomy 10.12)."

Lessons in Serving

ALTHOUGH Joan's academic record at college was not impressive, the record she left in the Christian Service Department told a different story. Every student at Columbia participated in supervised Christian service as part of his training.

During her first four terms, Joan led a Pioneer Girls' group on a housing estate. On the estate there was a community centre in which church and Sunday School were conducted on Sundays and a Pioneer Girls' club on a weekday. While Joan was there, more girls attended the club than at any time before or after. She seemed to have a way of drawing them to her. Most of the children were from broken homes. Perhaps because of her own home background Joan understood them and could help them better than anyone else.

Joan's part-time job while in college was tutoring a retarded girl, Ruth, playing games, going out for walks and picnics with her and teaching her the Bible. Joan took Ruth with her to her Pioneer Girls' group, and once Ruth's mother invited the group to a dinner party at her home, a lovely old colonial mansion with spacious rooms, thick rugs and fine furnishings. It was a new experience for the boisterous girls, untrained in manners, to visit such a home. They sat in awe around the long dining-table, set with fragile china, and were served in style by the maid. Joan, with her good humour and talent for organization, was able to keep everyone happy and everything under control, so that the dinner party was a great success all round. Joan had an inexhaustible fund of ideas, and of all the tutors Ruth had over the years, she loved Joan the best and never forgot her.

When Joan was assigned to lead a small Negro Bible club in a poor, underprivileged section of Columbia, so many children began to come to the club that they had to meet outside. Joan stood in the porch to speak to the boys and girls in the yard and on the pavement below, with adults, too, listening from the porches of surrounding houses. The youngsters felt her warm, loving interest and responded well to her teaching.

During her final term Joan taught a class of lively second formers in a large Negro school. Many years later one of the boys from this class shared his memories of Joan. ' Miss Killilea was very friendly and liked to have fun with me. Her lessons were very interesting and we didn't get sleepy listening to them. She put a lot of action in her stories and they always had good religious morals."

But Joan never took her success for granted and always spent a lot of time in preparation and prayer. At first she was afraid of work among the older girls and had a struggle with herself when asked to take a senior group at camp one summer, but finally accepted the responsibility. She recognized in this new assigment that God was promising help in an area where she was not naturally gifted; work with the younger girls was easy and natural to her. This was a further lesson in trusting and obedience.

She was despondent, too, when a girl in her cabin one year went home without accepting Christ; she felt as if she had failed. But God alone keeps accurate records and He alone knows how many young lives were influenced through Joan Killilea in Columbia and in the Maine and Pocono camps. Here is one girl's testimony, and it is no doubt typical of many:

"I became a believer while a Pilgrim at camp when Swiftie was my counsellor. I was having Morning Watch with her under an old apple tree on the hillside overlooking the lake. I don't remember much of what she said, but she told me about the best Friend she had, the Lord Jesus Christ. I accepted Christ as my Saviour then, although I never told anyone else until the next year."

This girl later became a club leader and camp counsellor herself.

Responding with Zeal

JOAN was unusually quiet as she sat one day with several other students in the college dining hall.

"What are you thinking about, Joan?" asked one of the fellows.

"Oh, I was just thinking about the missionary hymn we sang in chapel today, 'Ready to go, ready to stay'. You know, it's hard for me to sing that hymn honestly."

The others seemed surprised at Joan's frank admission. Then she added:

"I can gladly sing 'Ready to go', but I'm not so sure about singing 'Ready to stay' and really meaning it."

Ever since coming to Columbia Joan had become increasingly aware of her personal responsibility in God's programme to reach the world with the Gospel. During her first term she had written to friends:

"Every Sunday night the Foreign Missions Fellowship meets here. It has opened my eyes to thousands in the uttermost parts of the earth who are dying both physically and spiritually. We have prayer groups that cover the entire world and you go to the one of your choice. I do not know where the Lord will have me go for Him, whether at home or abroad, but He has led me to the China prayer group here. Only six out of 400 students attend this group, so we are like a little tug-boat, small but mighty. Of course, China is closed now, but there are many Christians behind the Bamboo Curtain who need prayer."

Gradually the conviction grew within Joan's heart that God was calling her to go to those who had never heard the Name of Jesus. Such verses as "For this cause have I raised thee up, for to shew in thee my power; and that my name may be declared throughout all the earth" came to her repeatedly.

Joan chose Galatians 1.15, 16 as her life verse: "It pleased God, who separated me from my mother's womb, and called me by his grace, to reveal his Son in me, that I might preach him among the heathen."

During the Christmas holidays, 1954, Joan attended the inter-varsity missionary convention in Urbana, Illinois.

"This visit was in the blueprint that God has for my life," Joan wrote afterwards. "Through the reading of the life of Hudson Taylor and other books, the Lord has given me a love for the China Inland Mission. There were many representatives of this Mission at Urbana and I had an interview with one of them. I told him of the love the Lord had given me for the Chinese people. He then asked that old touchy question:

" 'How old are you?'

"With a gulp I told him, 'Twenty-seven'.

"He seemed suprised and advised me to do one more year only at college. He thought two and a half years of Bible college was sufficient for me and that it would be better for me to get to the field before I was thirty, because the language and adjustment to the life there get harder the older you become. So now I am due to finish in '56. What then? Well, the Lord willing, I'll go to the candidates' course and sail that same year. Sail for where? This question I'm unable to answer, but He has that in His blueprint, too, and will reveal it to me in perfect time."

It appeared as though the desire that God had planted in Joan's heart while a child to work among Oriental children was to come to fruition. The China Inland Mission, no longer able to work in China, had opened fields in other Asian lands and changed its name to "Overseas Missionary Fellowship."

The following November, on Thanksgiving Day, Joan composed her letter of application to this Mission. She began:

"My heart is so full of thanksgiving and praise to our Lord and Saviour Jesus Christ on this Thanksgiving Day that I am sure that this is God's appointed time for me to write to you . . . It was just about three years ago that our Lord saw fit to draw me to Himself."

Joan continued the letter with a brief summary of her life. Then she added, "The Lord has wonderfully blessed me with a very strong and healthy body. To my knowledge I have never had to have the doctor, except, maybe, for childhood diseases. I believe that the Lord must have strenuous days ahead on the foreign field for me."

Finally, Joan told of God's call to her to missionary work and closed with the words, "I cannot keep this Friend to myself, I must go and share Him with those that have never heard the precious and glorious name of Jesus."

But along with the thrill of hearing God's call and responding, came times of humbling and testing, as she came to know herself better. "It seems that we are always so eager to share victories but not quite so eager to share the wickedness still left in our hearts. Seems as though each step becomes more difficult to take, each lesson harder to learn than the one before, each command a little harder to obey."

In a letter written during her last term, Joan told of testing in an area where young women are especially vulnerable. Word had just reached her of the engagement of her friend Roberta Schofield.

"Well, this is a successful leap year! Don't get excited – I don't mean for me, but for Berta! Certainly am happy for them both; now they'll be twice as effective for the Lord.

Have been having some real battles over that area in my life this term, especially the past few weeks. Have to be so careful that the evil one doesn't get a foothold, but at the same time, I don't want to miss what the Lord has for me. This Christmas someone said to me about a fellow student, 'Guess you won't pay any attention, but you ought to hang on to him.' I'm afraid I can't agree. I'm not sure if I ever mentioned this to you, but this fellow is only a second-year student and the Lord is sending me out now. Can't play around for two years while thousands are dying without Him. All I know is that His way is perfect and whether I go alone or otherwise, that's completely in His hands."

This zeal for missions sometimes led to misunderstandings. She was so overwhelmed by the needs of the mission field that she seemed to feel that all her friends should become missionaries, too. This, plus the fact that Joan tended to be impatient with Christians who did not reach her own standards, sometimes made others feel uncomfortable in her presence; they feared that they might not measure up to her expectations. The dean had noticed this "intolerance of the weaknesses of other Christians." Joan just could not understand how any Christian could do less than go all the way with the Lord. When a friend whom Joan had hoped would become a missionary, decided to marry an unbeliever, Joan urged her to change her mind, but her friend said nothing. When Joan found out that the girl was expecting a child she was utterly crushed. But through this experience she learned the importance of keeping her eyes fixed on Jesus Christ even though her friends might disappoint.

Joan was hard on herself as well as others. Sometimes she feared that she might go too far with her stunts and jokes and so dishonour the Lord or draw too much attention to herself. She went through brief periods when she became somewhat unnatural, trying to stifle her God-given humour and force herself into a "spiritual" mould.

Despite these "growing pains" each year as Joan returned to camp, old friends marvelled at the rapid growth in her Christian life. Some who had prayed for her salvation a few years before now turned to her for spiritual counsel.

Joan's time at Columbia came to a close in May, 1956, and there was manifestly a balance and a maturity about her Christian life. She expected to attend the candidates' course of the Overseas Missionary Fellowship in the autumn.

Meanwhile Joan devoted the summer months to the camps she loved – the first half of the summer to Pocono Cherith and the last half to Maine Cherith, and during that last summer in the States God used Joan in a most remarkable way to influence other lives for Himself.

The Oil of Love

IT was the first day of camp. A slim, attractive young counsellor stood at the bottom of the hill, filled with dread as she faced the responsibilities of a long camping season – her first experience at Camp Cherith.

"How can I live up to what is expected of me? Will the teenagers in my cabin accept me? Will I be able to give them the help they need?"

The counsellor's name was Dorothy Mainhood, a future colleague of Joan's in Thailand. She tells her own story:

"Suddenly I saw a redheaded counsellor bounding down the hill, laughing and talking with some campers she had in tow.

" 'Hullo,' called the redhead in a deep, friendly voice. 'My name's Swiftie. What's yours?'

" 'Brownie,' I replied. We walked into the dining hall together, and during the meal I began to feel the effects of Swiftie's infectious grin and buoyant spirit. My crushing fear of failure gradually lifted as I laughed at her cheerful humour.

"Swiftie seemed to have no fears whatever. She could cope with her own duties in camp and help others at the same time. I realized with relief that here was a warm heart and a helping hand for me, as well as for others who were having difficulty adjusting to camp life. In the following days we became good friends. Sometimes we had long chats together late in the evening after campers were tucked into bed. I opened up as never before, telling her all about myself – my fears and hopes and longings. Although I was a registered nurse and recent college graduate, I found myself talking to her as a child to an adult.

" 'No wonder the children love you,' I told her one day. 'I feel like one of them.'

"Once we had a day off together. It was raining and I felt as gloomy as the day. I couldn't seem to help my campers. How I longed for the same joyful, fruitful Christian life Joan had! That day this longing reached a terrible intensity. We did some shopping and then stopped for coffee. Suddenly she asked me,

" 'Why aren't you preparing to go to the mission field?'

"I thought to myself, 'What does that have to do with my depressed mood? Why does she have to ask me such awkward questions?' But I answered:

" 'Why should I rush? I've just finished college. I'm not ready to go yet.'

"My answer didn't seem to satisfy Swiftie. And her usual bright remarks to cheer me up were not forthcoming. She just let me wallow in my gloom. Then I asked her why she was in such a hurry to get to the mission field. By this time we had left the coffee shop and gone to a place on the mountain side where we tried to build a fire for a barbecue. But it only smouldered because the wood was damp. So we sat there by the smoke while Joan took out her green leather-bound Bible and opened it at Ezekiel 34. There hadn't been much conversation all the way out to this place, and now she said very deliberately and with definite authority, 'This is why I'm going now.' And she began to read. As she read the fourth verse the voice of God Himself spoke clearly through her Boston accent:

" 'The diseased have ye not strengthened, neither have ye healed that which was sick, neither have ye bound up that which was broken, neither have ye brought again that which was driven away, neither have ye sought that which was lost . . . '

"Never before had I heard God's voice speak so clearly to me, although I have heard it many times since. Joan seemed to know God so well – it was as if she were looking at a tree close up, but I was looking at it from a distance. I couldn't see the leaves and branches as she could – just the outline. Now suddenly there was God, close up to me, too. I knew if I would be willing to go to those who were without a Shepherd He would continue to be real to me and this vital, joyful Christian life would be for me, too. So I told Him I would go, and we prayed together. I don't know how long we meditated over those verses, but I do know that God broke into my life that day and laid His hand on me, and I have never been the same since.

"Finally, we decided it was too wet to build a fire, so we drove on. We came to a sandy strip of land and there in the middle of nowhere was a big fire burning. Apparently, someone had been clearing the land of old wood and left it burning on the sand. Swiftie said,

" 'See the Lord had a fire all ready for us all the time !'

"I was never so thrilled. To think that He knew that we needed a fire and had led us to the right place to find it ! It was like visible evidence that He is able to do anything for His children. The food was especially delicious, the sunset most beautiful, and I had never experienced such peace of heart.

"That evening I realized that I knew nothing at all about Swiftie, although I'd talked non-stop all about myself and she had helped me so much. So I asked her to tell me of her life. Then I heard the most remarkable story of God's love and transforming power that I had ever heard. It made me so ashamed. I'd had so much of family love and security, so much opportunity in life, yet I had known so little of the Lord. She had had none of these, yet she had the most vital real relationship with God I'd ever seen.

"The rest of the summer was filled with rich, satisfying experiences. Instead of the terrible longing whch came when I heard Swiftie's camp fire messages on the need for complete dedication to the Lord, I, too, was able to give meaningful messages.

"But still the campers' needs were not always met. I was especially upset about one girl, Barbara, who came from a big city gang. I wasn't able to touch her life; she simply did not respond. One day, while talking with Swiftie about her, I sat down on the side of the hill and the tears fell. Swiftie put her hand on my shoulder and said;

" 'You can never meet the needs of these girls, Brownie. All you can do, and all the Lord wants you to do, is to love them and pray for them.'

"How many times since then I've remembered those few words of advice! I knew she was right – yet I wondered how she could bear so cheerfully the burden of others' spiritual needs. Not many days later, Barbara went home, and that afternoon I went to the counsellors' cabin during a free hour. There I found Swiftie praying for Barbara; she was weeping with great hard sobs that shook her whole body. I knew then how great her concern for others was, but she was casting her burden on the Lord who alone is able to bear it."

Later, in Thailand, Dorothy Mainhood and Joan often spent their vacations together, and through the years their friendship deepened. Nor was Dorothy the only one Joan influenced in the direction of the mission field. Others are in Africa and South America today.

Occasionally it happened that a counsellor came to camp to serve, but soon realized that she herself did not really belong to the Lord. This was the case with Jan Cleveland, who came to Maine Camp Cherith to counsel in a Pilgrim cabin for a week. Swiftie was her senior. Jan observed Swiftie closely that week, just as Swiftie had observed others at that same camp some years before.

"It didn't take long to realize that Swiftie really cared about people, especially her Pilgrim campers. I liked girls, too, but I didn't feel deeply concerned about them. They made me pretty impatient when they talked and giggled during rest hour. But Swiftie loved them and really listened to them with an ear that was open to hear their deepest need, disguised beneath their chatter. I discovered, quite by accident, that she kept a 5 a.m. appointment with her Lord to tell Him about their needs.

"And, of course, there was her wonderful sense of humour and her gay abandonment to the world of make-believe. As Peter Pan she made the campers gasp as she swung down on a rope from the rafters high in the dining hall to rescue Wendy from the terrible Captain Hook! One rainy day she dressed up as a TV personality and recruited talented campers. As she made endless pots of tea she would introduce 'new talent' in her own whimsical way. I laughed until I cried at her quick Irish humour, so gentle with others yet able to laugh with us at her own foibles.

"This life continued to speak to me all week long. When young I had had little exposure to church. I had gone through nurses' training convinced that if there was a God, He was not concerned for me, and persuaded that the Bible, at best, was a collection of myths. Since marriage and the birth of a son and daughter my attitude had become a searching one. For two years I had been under an evangelical ministry and had even become an assistant guide in a Pioneer Girls' club. I had acquired a head knowledge of the Lord Jesus Christ, but in this week at camp I was discovering how very far my heart was from Him.

"One night I went outside after the campers were asleep and lay on my back on the hillside, looking up at the stars. The crushing realization came that I was alone and very lost.

"Friday came, and I was due to go home on Saturday morning. All the staff were busy completing badge requirements with girls and filing camp reports. I knew Swiftie was deeply involved with her responsibilities, but I ventured a remark that I had a 'little problem' I would like to discuss. How can I ever thank the Lord enough that Swiftie was close to Him and cared enough to remember my need after her campers were tucked in for the night and before she started several hours' work on reports! She came to my cabin and discovered that my 'little problem' was that I had never asked the Lord to forgive my sin and come into my heart; I don't know how long we sat there on the edge of my cot. The campers slept quietly while a battle raged within my soul, for by this time I had prepared quite a mental list of reasons for not making a decision just then. Swiftie listened patiently, then quietly and gently led me to her dearest Friend. I met Him there for the first time, and He worked His miracle of power and love and peace in my heart.

"This might have been the lovely ending of the story, but it is not. The Lord opened the way for me to return to camp a week later as the camp nurse, and I stayed for the final two weeks. During this time my family was there, too, and they came to know and love Swiftie and in due course to know and love her Lord."

Swiftie's friendship with Jan continued throughout her years in Thailand. When God gave the Clevelands a new baby girl, the older children wanted her to be named Joan. How thrilled the older Joan was when she came on furlough in 1961 and met her little namesake!

What was the secret of Swiftie's influence? Jan says, "As I review the years of our friendship and re-read her letters, there is one overwhelming impression, that of love – the uncomplicated winsome love of the Lord Jesus, shining through an individual who had taken Him completely at His Word."

Thus God had proved to Swiftie that He could use her to "reveal His Son" to others in America. But she longed for the day when her life verse (Galatians 1.15, 16) would become reality and He would reveal His Son in and through her to the heathen – to those who had not yet heard His Name.

Obeying His Call

The Master calls! Shall not my heart
In warm responsive love reply
"Lord, here am I, send me, send me –
Thy willing slave – to live or die:
An instrument unfit indeed
Yet Thou wilt give me what I need."

E. May Grimes[1]

WITH great excitement Joan mounted the steps of the OMF mission home on West School House Lane in Philadelphia. She had long looked forward to this day,

[1] Joan chose this poem for her prayer card.

C

but now it was here she found herself a bit apprehensive, for she was about to begin the eight-week candidates' course. Suppose the Mission leaders should decide at the end of eight weeks that she wasn't missionary material after all?

Joan pushed this unpleasant thought aside as she opened the heavy door and entered the aristocratic old building. She was greeted by a secretary who showed her round the offices, the book-store, and the publications department, and then led her along a corridor on the second floor.

"We call this corridor 'the Burma road'. It leads to the part of the building which you will be sharing with nineteen other candidates for the next two months."

Joan had time to browse around, getting acquainted with her new surroundings. She loved the spacious, comfortable atmosphere and the tasteful furnishings. In the lower hall stood a curio cupboard, and scattered throughout the rooms were lamps, pictures and other objects from the Orient – all reminders of the Far East for whose millions the Mission exists. In the living room Joan discovered a large wall map of South-East Asia.

"This is where classes and prayer meetings are held," she was told.

When Joan entered the attractive dining-room, her attention was drawn to a huge portrait of Hudson Taylor, the founder of the Mission, hanging over the mantlepiece. She thought of the giants of the faith who had once walked here and perhaps sat at the massive oak table in the centre of the room – James Fraser, pioneer missionary to Lisuland; missionary writer, Isobel Kuhn; John and Betty Stam, martyrs in China, and others. The Scripture texts on the wall reminded her of the One whose power brought the Mission into being and sustains it to this day. Gratitude welled up in Joan's heart for the privilege of being a candidate here.

Soon Joan met the other candidates and the course was in full swing. Mornings were spent in classes, and afternoons and evenings were devoted to studies. There was much to learn about the history and policies of the Mission and the countries in which it works. Each day at 4 p.m. a volleyball game gave opportunity to stretch cramped muscles. There were interviews with Mission leaders, injections (Joan began to feel like a pin cushion!), papers to fill out, passports to be obtained, speaking engagements at week-ends, plus teas and suppers at the homes of members of the Mission. It was a full schedule and the weeks flew past.

One day Joan stood reading her mail during a pause in the time-table. Suddenly she gave a cry of joy.

"Listen to this!" she said, "The Pioneer Girls' board has chosen me to be their sixth missionary. Isn't that exciting?"

Joan had trouble concentrating on her studies the rest of the day, so thrilled was she over this news. She had asked God to give her a few children to be her prayer partners. Now she had 27,000 girls who would support her in prayer as well as with their gifts.

On November 5 the great day arrived. One by one the candidates appeared before the Council for their final interview. Joan's turn came at last and she was officially accepted as a member of the Mission family. Two days later the commissioning service was held, and Joan was one of the three candidates chosen to give her testimony.

During the following months she travelled to many states visiting Pioneer Girls' groups, so that her young supporters could get a personal glimpse of her and hear her testimony. The story of her long search before finally finding peace in Christ made a deep impression everywhere. There were also humorous occasions. After speaking of all the things she had tried during her quest for happiness – pretty clothes, a car, her own house, parties – Swiftie often asked the girls if any of them could tell her what would really make her happy. Once a young listener answered, "A husband!"

"Well, suppose I had a husband and still was not happy?"

Another girl raised her hand eagerly and said, "Have a baby!"

Swiftie suppressed her laughter and decided not to put that question again!

Finally, on February 28, 1957, the s.s. Ryndam of the Holland-America Line sailed into the Atlantic with nineteen missionaries aboard and a senior missionary, J. Morris Rockness, and his wife. Joan's thoughts, as she stood on the deck laden with flower gifts, travelled to the Pioneer Girls' motto "Looking unto Jesus". In a letter to friends she wrote, "I could see just a glimpse of what it must have meant for Him to leave His home in glory in obedience to His Father's will. Yes, and to travel the very same road that I was about to undertake – for was not our lovely Lord Jesus a foreign missionary who travelled much of His life alone? It was because of Him that I was going forth; it was He who had first loved me and had given Himself for me."

"Gong-gong-gong" went the signal for dinner. Little did Joan realize that it would be the first and last meal on board ship that she would really enjoy! But she describes her arrival with the party in England more cheerfully,

"At last land was sighted and it was none other than Ireland. Sure an' with a last name like mine, you can be certain I got rather excited to see the old country.

"Next we arrived in jolly ol' England. As we descended the gang-plank there stood a 'bobby' with his high round hat and handlebar moustache. Quick as a flash, a porter breezed by and spoke – 'Be right with ya, love.' Soon we were on the train to London. Never will I forget the message which greeted me as I got off the train – a sign which read 'Mind the gap'. Immediately I thought of Ezekiel 22.30: 'And I sought for a man among them, that should make up the hedge, and stand in the gap before me for the land, that I should not destroy it: but I found none.' I used this message frequently to challenge the folk in England. As I go forth to stand in the gap, they must mind the gap with prayer. Nor shall I ever forget the night I spoke at the main British valedictory meeting in Birmingham. How thankful I was for the peace He gave, as I looked into 2,000 faces . . .

"We left England on April 4 aboard the s.s. Chusan. One month at sea. The Creator and His creation became more wonderful. I never thought I would see the night when the sky could be more beautiful than it was at New England, Camp Cherith, but it happened in the Indian Ocean . . . Due to the Suez crisis we had to take the long route via the Cape. The days were often very hot, but the swimming pool was always refreshing after basking in the sun. Competitive games such as deck tennis, deck quoits, and table tennis kept us all busy. One day we had aquatic sports, for which I entered. In the pillow fight on the greasy pole I had a fifty-pound advantage over my opponent, and so won the prize.

"Then there was the night of the fancy-dress party. One of the missionaries dressed up as an organ-grinder and I went as his monkey. It was good for many a laugh, but I could hardly move for days afterwards due to all the jumping around I had done. But we won the prize and so it was worth the few aches and pains.

"We also had a wonderful time with the children, holding Sunday School and day classes for them . . . On May 2 we reached Singapore."

New Sounds and Customs

JOAN sat at her desk at the OMF Language Centre in Singapore, composing her first prayer letter to the Pioneer Girls. It was evening and a gentle breeze brought welcome relief from the damp, sticky heat of the day. She found it hard to concentrate, for the nights and sounds of Singapore were still new and exhilarating.

Singapore, a modern westernized city in the heart of the Far East, is the site of the international headquarters of the Overseas Missionary Fellowship. On a quiet, shady street, away from the bustle of the city, stand the attractive modern buildings of the Language Centre where thirty-one new workers, ten British, nineteen North Americans and two South Africans, were to receive their initial orientation.

Sitting before the open window Joan could see the distant lights of tall apartment buildings and the flickering headlights of cars and buses. But on Chancery Lane all was relatively quiet and peaceful. Tall trees and tropical foliage cast their deep shadows. The only sounds besides the muffled roar of the distant traffic were the chirping of insects and the voices of passers-by. The birds which had sung so heartily all day were apparently asleep, and even the street vendors with their ringing bells had gone home for the night. The heavy fragrance of the frangipani tree drifted in on the breeze, tempting Joan to go out to gather some of the white waxy blossoms which had fallen to the ground.

Joan jerked her thoughts back to her letter. "What shall I write? There's so much to tell them about life out here. But how to put it down on paper?" She reviewed in her mind the experiences of the past weeks. Shortly after arrival, Joan and the other missionaries had been interviewed by the Mission Directors and given their field designations. In reaching these important decisions the needs on the various fields, the health, talents and language aptitude of the missionary, and also his own conviction as to God's leading, were all taken into account. Joan had been particularly interested in the work among the tribes of North Thailand, but she was happy to accept her appointment to Central Thailand, for this was still Thailand, the land to which she felt especially drawn. The new missionaries were to remain in Singapore for four and a half months of classes, including instruction in the language of the countries to which they were assigned.

At last the idea for the prayer letter came to her. She would describe a day at the Language Centre.

"6 a.m. Do you hear someone running from room to room, letting the swinging doors fly in and out? Well, don't be frightened; it's only our human alarm clock. There certainly seems to be a reluctant thump of feet on the linoleum floors, but then it takes a little time to get disentangled from our mosquito nets. These old eyes just don't like to open to the brightness of the electric light in the dark dawn, but daylight comes quickly. Can you hear the chorus of crowing roosters? (I think there are as many chickens as people in Singapore). We must be very quiet until breakfast time because everybody is spending time with the Lord Jesus. We need Him so very much to undertake for us in our language study. How good it is to know that He is the only true Instructor!

"7 a.m. Ding-dong-dong. Time for breakfast. It's very much as at home, except the bananas have just been cut off the trees in our garden. After breakfast we have family prayers. There are thirty-one of us in language school, and we all take a turn in leading. One day I shared what the Lord had been teaching me about John 20.21, 'As my Father hath sent me, even so send I you.'

"8.30 brings room-cleaning time. We must be sure

to check our books for mildew and air our bedding that gets so musty-smelling.

"9–12. The morning is spent in studying vocabulary, learning grammar, listening to tape recordings, and individual study with our teachers. We have both a man and a woman teacher, which is good because the Thai people use a different ending on their sentences according to the sex of the speaker.

"12 noon. Chinese dinner. Hope you don't have as much trouble as I do managing chopsticks. After dinner comes mail – that is, if there is any. Then comes one of my favourite times of the day – siesta!

"3–5 p.m. This time is spent learning Thai script, memorizing John 3.16 and Acts 4.12, and the Thai alphabet which has forty-four consonants and twenty-eight vowels or vowel clusters. What a thrill it is to hear the Word of God in a strange tongue, which will one day be very precious to someone that has never heard the name of Phra-jesu!

"5 p.m. Volleyball. We get a little warm playing, even though the sun is going down and the court is in the shade. There is just time for a quick shower before supper.

"7.30–10 p.m. Three evenings a week we have meetings. The others are spent relaxing, letter writing or preparing for Sunday School. I have a class of English-speaking Chinese girls. Their problems are the same as those of teenagers in the States. How thankful I am to share God's precious Word! Sun Moon Lee has just made a profession of faith. Won't you pray for her? It has been fun to go hiking or picnicing on Saturdays with them, even though they speak Chinese most of the time. One day, when we were playing a guessing game, they kept yelling 'Four feet'. After trying to guess the meaning I finally had to ask them.

" 'Well, if you don't guess correctly, you have to sing a

song, or tell a story, or do something – you know – pay
a forfeet (forfeit).'

"10 p.m. Bedtime already. Our house is built for the
tropics with plenty of open space to allow air to circulate
freely and keep us cool. There are open spaces above the
partitions between the rooms, the same light even shines
in all the rooms, so we must turn all the lights out on time.
Be sure to tuck the edges of your mosquito net under
your camp cot mat before you go to sleep. The sheets
seem a little damp tonight from the moisture in the air,
but I like them that way because they make me think
I'm at camp. (How I missed being there this summer!)
Do you hear that funny little noise? It's just the little
house lizards saying 'Good-night'. They are helpful room-
mates, for they eat up any insects that come within their
range.

"The day has gone quickly. Must say 'Good-night'
now. It's been fun having you here."

Joan found the language more difficult than she had
anticipated. Especially unsettling was the fact that most
of the others seemed to find it less difficult than she did
and were making faster progress. Yet she had not found
her studies easy at Columbia, either, and God had helped
her then. Surely He would not fail her now.

As the course in Singapore came to an end, Joan prepared
for the three-day boat journey to Bangkok, Thailand.
In late 1957, with eager anticipation she and several other
missionaries boarded a coastal cargo vessel and sailed
up the Gulf of Siam. When they reached the mouth
of the Chao Phraya river they had to wait at the bar until
the tide was high enough for the ship to cross. As they
steamed up the river towards Bangkok the travellers stood
on deck, straining to catch their first glimpse of Thai
life – the Thai houses built on stilts extending out over
the river and the people squatting at their little piers,
washing clothes or dishes or jumping into the river to

take a bathe. The Thais love the convenience of living along the waterways, and many of them live in houseboats.

Thailand, formerly known as Siam, means "Land of the Free". Thailand maintained its political independence all through the centuries when neighbouring countries became European colonies. But though Thailand was free from foreign control, there was little freedom for the individual in a feudal system of government headed by a king with absolute power. Toward the close of the last century, many political and social reforms were introduced by King Chulalongkorn and since 1932 the Government has been a constitutional monarchy. Joan was interested to learn that the present king was born in her home state of Massachusetts, where his father was a student at Harvard University at the time, and that he still speaks Thai with a slight American accent!

Spiritually, the millions living in the "Land of the Free" are still in bondage, for among approximately thirty million, less than 30,000 know the Son of God who alone can free from the power of sin, death and hell. Although missionaries have witnessed in parts of Thailand for over 100 years, the central provinces had no Christian churches and almost no modern hospitals when the Overseas Missionary Fellowship began work there in 1952. This area is in the basin of the Chao Phraya river system and constitutes the rich rice bowl of Thailand. Joan counted it a privilege to be among those bringing the gospel into this region, where the colourful Buddhist religion has held undisputed sway for centuries.

Nearing Bangkok, the river traffic increased. There were swift canoes, roomy sampans and quaint junks as well as bigger ocean-going freighters and cargo vessels. Women with broad-brimmed straw hats paddled boats loaded with fresh fruits and vegetables to Bangkok's famous floating market. There were even floating restaurants – small boats on which rice, soups and coffee are heated over charcoal braziers.

The excitement mounted within her as Joan tried to take in all the strange new sights and sounds.

"Just think – this is Bangkok! I can hardly believe we're actually here!"

"It's easy to see why it's called the Venice of the East," said one of the men of the party. "Have you noticed the many *klong* (canals) that branch off from the river? And say, take a look at those glittering *wat* (temple) spires over there." The new missionary obviously enjoyed showing off a few words of Thai.

As the boat docked the Field Superintendent and business manager of the Mission were on the wharf to greet the new arrivals, help them with their baggage and escort them to the OMF home.

Bangkok is a mixture of ancient and modern. Narrow lanes lined with simple teakwood houses contrasted with the wide main streets and the modern hotels and office buildings. Traffic is a hopeless snarl of cars, buses, bicycles and push-carts.

"And what in the world is that strange vehicle?" Joan asked, "the one that looks like an enormous tricycle?" It had a seat for two over the two back wheels and was pedalled by a man wearing shorts and a straw sun-hat.

The older missionary smiled. "That's a *samlor* – sort of glorified rickshaw. You'll find them quite convenient as taxis."

Most fascinating of all were the people. There were Indian women in saris; Chinese women in black trousers and wide hats, balancing shoulder poles with loaded baskets dangling from each end; pretty Thai girls in gay flowered *pasins* (wrap-around skirts) and white blouses; young women in western clothing; old grannies with cropped hair and teeth stained from chewing the juicy betel nut; bare-bottomed babies; plump, wealthy Chinese merchants; tonsured Buddhist monks, conspicuous in bright saffron yellow robes; and street vendors cooking over charcoal braziers.

The new arrivals finally reached the OMF Mission Home, where they were to spend another three months of language study before proceeding to their centres. There was great value in getting acquainted with Bangkok, the capital, before moving up-country, for Bangkok is literally the heart of Thai life – home of the king, seat of the Government and the centre of culture. Progressive young people flock to Bangkok seeking education, better careers and higher salaries. Although Bangkok is not typical of Thailand as a whole, its influence is widely felt in the land.

During the next few weeks Joan learned more about the Thai life around her. She observed the monks going from door to door in the early morning carrying rice bowls, into which housewives placed food in the belief that they were thus earning merit for the next life. "No wonder Thailand is called 'Land of the Yellow Robe'! " thought Joan. "The monks are everywhere." She discovered that most young men in Thailand spend three months in the monastery. Even the king had done so. Some remain monks for life.

Joan also visited some of the 300 Buddhist temples in Bangkok alone, beautiful structures, elaborate and ornate with chalk-white stucco walls, steep gabled roofs of shiny orange and green tiles, and gracefully gilded spires. They enshrine statues of Buddha – standing, sitting or reclining, the most sacred of them being the Emerald Buddha, made of a solid piece of green jasper. Only twenty inches tall, this image rests on an altar thirty feet high. At the beginning of each new season – hot, rainy, cool, in a traditional ceremony the king changes the robes on the Buddha.

Joan found it difficult to appreciate the artistic beauty of the temples and images, for her heart ached to see people bowing down before idols. "They have mouths, but they speak not: eyes have they, but they see not: they have ears, but they hear not" (Psalm 115.5, 6).

Although Buddha never claimed to be a god and Buddhist scholars say that the statues are only memorials to their great teacher and reminders of his doctrines, the vast majority of the people actually worship the Buddha images. Traces of Hindu mythology and spirit-worship are also mingled with their religion. Almost every home has its little spirit house on a post in the rear, like an ornate bird table. In the country, Thai farmers worship at shrines for the earth goddess or the rice goddess.

As Joan became aware of the grip of idolatry on the Thai people, she longed to tell them of a living Saviour who could forgive their sins, One who could hear and answer their prayers. But before she could do this, she faced two major problems – identification and communication. She had to identify with the people, learn their customs and ways of doing things before they would accept her and listen to her message. She also had to acquire the language well enough to communicate this message. Joan applied herself to these twin tasks. Language study was laborious and slow, but her love for people helped her overcome the cultural barrier. She found the Thai congenial and friendly. Small, with golden skin, brown eyes and black hair, they were quite a contrast to Joan with her sturdy build, red hair, blue eyes and fair skin. She often found herself the centre of attention, especially in the country where *farang* (foreigners) were not so familiar a sight as in the city. She once said:

"I feel as if I'm perpetually on TV!"

The Thai are quiet-spoken, gentle, and easy-going, and Joan was thankful that she had learned to curb her own boisterousness at college.

Newcomers soon learn to use the Thai form of greeting, called the *"wai"*. The Thai do not shake hands, but put their hands together and hold them to the chin, the nose or the forehead, according to how much respect should be shown.

In Thailand the head is revered and the feet are considered unworthy. Older missionaries warned, "Remember, it is an insult to point with your foot or to touch or reach over a person's head. When you shop at the market where wares are spread out on the ground, don't point at the item you want with your toe, or the salesman may turn away and refuse to wait on you. Never even refer to your feet in conversation unless you first say, 'Excuse me'. In a railway carriage, never reach over a person's head to take down your luggage before saying 'Excuse me', then wait until the person gives permission or moves out of your way. Also, remember, ladies never cross their legs in Thailand!"

Joan often found herself on the verge of breaking one of these rules, but gradually these customs became a part of her behaviour.

The three months in Bangkok passed all too quickly. Joan was then assigned to Chainat, a small provincial town further north. She was by no means finished with language study, but in Chainat she would have more opportunity to use the language in visiting and meetings. "At last I'll be doing real missionary work!"

In December, 1957, she made the four-hour journey by train and bus to her new home.

Beginning the Work

ON the northbound train Joan observed the landscape of Central Thailand – flat rice fields stretching out in every direction, broken only by small villages half hidden by tall trees and thick shrubs. In December, the rice fields are a golden brown and the early crops are being harvested by farmers wearing flat-topped, wide brimmed straw hats. There were children riding on water buffaloes or bathing them in the river. These animals are used both for ploughing the rice fields in the spring and for threshing the rice at harvest-time. Now and then Joan caught a glimpse of elephants, also used as work animals and trained to haul the teak logs out of the forests, particularly in the north.

At Chainat the Mission had rented a second house to accommodate the additional workers of whom Joan was one. The house was said to be haunted by an evil spirit and no Thai would live in it. Joan wrote:

"The most popular question I'm asked here is 'Aren't you afraid?' Afraid of what? Well, it's the house I'm living in. It looks just like all the other houses in our little town, but everyone says an evil spirit lives in it. Some claim to have seen it. If you were to travel around Thailand you would find a spirit house in almost every yard. The family puts out flowers and food to please the spirits so they won't enter the house to cause sickness and death. The spirit house for our home stands just outside my bedroom window. We aren't allowed to take it down because we only rent the property. When we moved into this house, the first thing we had to do was knock down the spirit shelf and tear a red and white cloth from every beam where it had been nailed to keep the spirits out. I wish you could have seen the expressions on the faces of the children as they watched. The big brown eyes just about popped out of their heads, and one little three-year-old girl clung tightly to her big brother. How thankful I was for the Word the Lord spoke to me that first night as I was reading Psalm 4.8, 'I will both lay me down in peace, and sleep: for thou, Lord, only makest me dwell in safety'.

"Come now and let me show you round a Thai house

on stilts. First of all you must remove your shoes before
climbing the ladder to enter. Now see the lovely teak
wood flooring laid with spaces between the planks to let
the breeze blow through. The shine on the floor is not
shellac but the result of polishing by many bare feet. The
house has no painted woodwork or papered walls, but
just the bare wood. We have electricity from dark until
midnight, but most of the time it isn't very strong so we
have to use kerosene lanterns. In the mornings when I
get up it's still dark, so my little lantern comes in handy
then, too. In our house we have a little furniture, but
most Thai country people use none at all. They sit and
sleep on grass mats on the floor and literally eat off the
floor, too. That is, they eat out of dishes set on a mat
or tray on the floor. Unlike some other Eastern people,
Thais use a spoon and fork rather than chopsticks. They
may have a cabinet for their clothes, but they don't need
a store cupboard for food or a refrigerator because they
buy their food one day at a time. That pail-shaped clay
object in the corner is the charcoal stove. Yes, it's big
enough because all we eat is rice and hot, peppery curry
sauce.

"We don't have running water in our house but there
is a lovely big bath tub at the end of the street – the river!
In the rainy season we catch water from the tin roof and
store it in big water jars – just like those of Bible times –
so that for a time we can take our bath on the back porch
by just pouring a pail of water over ourselves and letting
the water drain through the cracks in the floor.

"Can you hear the children running up the street,
shouting, 'We're going to the house of Jesus' and listen
to the passer-by who stops to read aloud the sign we
have on the front porch – 'Jesus said, Fear not. Believe on
the Lord Jesus Christ and thou shalt be saved.'?

"Come and visit us in our little house whenever you're
over this way, won't you?"

When Joan heard that even the policeman was afraid to pass the haunted house at night, she said, "Just for fun I'd like to drape myself in a sheet and appear on the porch some night as the policeman passes by." But of course she didn't!

Adjusting to the Thai way of living was not always easy. Despite her efforts to identify, many barriers remained. "No matter how hard we try to become identified with the people," Joan wrote, "there is still the constant feeling of being the rich foreigner. The very fact that I wear glasses shows I'm rich, and much as I'd like to discard them it's an impossibility. Yet the living standard in Thailand is high for Asia."

Adjusting to the climate was another problem, for the tropical heat is enervating. There are three distinct seaons in Thailand – the stifling hot, dry season from March to May, the rainy season with daily showers and frequent floods from June to October, and the cool season from November to February.

Progress in the language was painfully slow and, as is usual with all who learn a new language, accompanied by some embarrassing mistakes. Thai is a tonal language with five tones, so that a drop or rise in the voice makes the difference between two words that are otherwise alike. Once Joan interrupted herself in the middle of a letter:

"Flash – here's a 'right on the spot' funny story regarding language. Just a few minutes ago three little children came in from the school next door to see a poster on our wall called 'The Two Ways' to heaven and hell. I explained to these little gals that in hell there is fire. The Thai word is *fy*, but the word for water buffalo happens to be *qwhy* which some Thai people pronounce *fy*. So after my explanation one little girl looked at me and said, 'Oh, are the water buffaloes in hell just like those that went down the street?' "

In spite of similar mistakes Joan was constantly using the language in a limited way.

"Words cannot express the thrill of telling someone about the Lord Jesus when he has never even heard His name. My senior, Grace Harris, and I go to a children's meeting across the river every Sunday afternoon. It's way out in the country, and when the children spot the boat coming they shout to all the neighbours, 'Jesus has come!' Isn't that a heart-searching greeting? How I long for them to receive Him as readily as they receive us!"

Her colleagues at Chainat felt that Joan made a great contribution to the children's work even before she could speak much Thai, through her love for them, her bright and winning ways with them and her endless fund of ideas and plans.

Joan purchased a bicycle with money she had received as a Christmas gift from Pioneer Girls. Writing to the Pioneer Girls' clubs she said,

"I'd like you to meet my new bike. Its name is *Poo-nam-tang,* which is Thai for 'pioneer'. What better name could it have, seeing that it comes from Pioneer Girls and seeing that it's going to be used to pioneer into places where people have never heard the precious name of Jesus?"

On a hot sunny morning not long afterward, Joan wheeled *Poo-nam-tang* out into the street and rode over to the other mission house. There Grace was waiting, and the two started out on Joan's first bicycle preaching tour.

Grace, her light brown hair combed neatly into two side buns, was English, but had grown up in Japan, where her parents had been missionaries. She had spent a term in China before the door closed and she and Joan shared a common interest in children's work.

The two women rode along the main road out of Chainat until they reached a narrow track through the rice fields. Harvest was over and the soil was sun-baked and bare.

"Wait until you see these fields in the summer. They're like an ocean of rippling green," said Grace.

As they approached a wooded area, Joan asked:

"Are there villages back in those woods?"

"O yes, hundreds of them," Grace replied. "You can't see them from the main road, but they're there."

It was a relief when they reached the forest of bamboo, palm, coconut and banana trees which sheltered them from the hot sun. Eventually they reached a small settlement of houses – simple, unpainted teak dwellings with steeply slanting roofs. Most Thai farmers own their own land, and keep their wooden ploughs and other farm implements under the houses. Loud barking of dogs announced the arrival of the two *farang* ladies.

"Are we going to stop here?" asked Joan, looking nervously at the snarling, fierce-looking dogs coming at her from all sides.

"We'll just keep going until we see some people. They'll probably invite us to come and sit under their houses to cool off," replied Grace.

Sure enough, a family invited them to come and sit down, calling off the dogs as the two missionaries alighted from their bikes. Stepping carefully over pigs, ducks, chickens and children, they found a spot to sit down. Joan tried to converse with the people but was not yet able to give a talk. This Grace did. Twice during her message one of the women interrupted to ask their age and other personal questions. Joan made a mental note that next time she would give them this information in advance, so that they would concentrate better on the Truth being taught.

As the missionaries prepared to leave, one man said, "Why didn't you come before with this good news? I have never heard it."

The words echoed in Joan's mind the rest of the morning and all the way back through the forest and rice fields.

Writing to Ruth that evening she said, "Coming out here and seeing the tremendous needs of people who have been denied hearing about the Lord Jesus, I just wonder how much longer He will withhold judgment on those who say they know Him but will not share Him."

Joan and Grace had been invited to teach English in a school, using the Bible as their textbook.

"Every Thursday the headmaster takes us to dinner after the lesson, and this gives us an opportunity to speak with him. His heart certainly seems to have been prepared by the Lord. Two weeks ago we gave him a Bible and he was not the least embarrassed about it. In fact he showed it to the chief of police whom we met in the market. This week he came to visit us and had read eleven chapters in his Bible. He says he believes in his heart that this teaching is the truth, but because of his position it is difficult for him to be anything but Buddhist outwardly. Then he added:

" 'I guess if I really believed in my heart I would want to have a Christian school.'

"Possibly he is already a secret believer. Won't you pray that if he is, he may take a bold stand for our Lord and Saviour Jesus Christ?

"The Lord seems to be working in the hearts of some of the students because the headmaster told us that twelve students no longer bow to Buddha in morning worship. Answers to an exam question were an encouragement to my heart. 'I will obey Jesus,' 'I will follow Jesus,' 'I have believed in Jesus.' Truly the Lord has opened the door, and we are standing on His promise that no man shall shut it until He has called out students for Himself."

One of the most fruitful aspects of the Chainat work was the ministry among leprosy patients.

"Every Monday morning we travel about twenty-five miles by bus to hold a clinic in a *sala,* a simple shelter consisting of a thatched roof set up on poles. Every Tuesday morning we have a clinic here in Chainat when I go to help sing and count pills, and sometimes I even tell one of my stories or play Gospel records. They are such dear people and many have come to love the Lord. You'd love to hear them say they don't care about the deformity of their bodies now because one day they will have new bodies. How wonderful to see them try to turn the pages of their Bibles with their stumps of hands! They wrap their Bibles all up in rags to keep them clean."

Despite her busy schedule, Joan took time to go around to get acquainted with the shopkeepers and neighbours. When she could not express herself in Thai, she used English, and the Thais sensed her friendliness even though they did not always understand her. She made friends in the dressmaker's shop, the hairdresser's shop, the "coke" shops and everywhere. Her special friend was four-year-old "Cupcake", a lovable little neighbour with whom Joan was not shy to use Thai and from whom she learned a lot not found in books.

Although Joan managed to restrain her natural exuberance to avoid offending the gentle Thai people, she did not entirely succeed. One night before going to bed she danced a little Irish jig in the "privacy" of her room just for fun. Apparently a little boy was peeping through the cracks in the walls and the next day he asked Joan's co-worker:

"Can *you* dance like Kulab?"

Joan's Thai name, Kulab, means "Rose", which was her real middle name.

All things considered, despite the many adjustments, Joan found her first six months in Chainat very satisfying. Writing in May, 1959, she said:

"Life is great here in Thailand. I love it. The weather is hot – 108° in the shade today, but one gets used to it. The rainy season is due, when things will cool off a little. It will then rain every day, but only in the late afternoon for a couple of hours, just enough to fill up the water jars. Eating Thai food hasn't bothered me at all. In fact I now like it. It's mostly rice with a hot curry of some type on it. I love the many different fruits.

"The people are as happy-go-lucky as you can imagine. Their most popular expression is *'Mai pen rai'*, which means 'Oh, never mind', said with a shrug of the shoulders. If you want to buy a pair of sandals and they don't have your size, they just give you the closest size to it and say, 'Oh, never mind – it's all right.' If you want to travel somewhere you never know how long it will take, because the old bus chugs along the bumpy road (just like the road into camp) and then stops for anyone who has a little shopping to do or wants to eat. Sometimes you sit in a village for an hour and a half until there are enough people – and animals – on the bus to make the trip worth while. Life in Thailand is really nonchalant!"

But Joan was not nonchalant about her purpose for being in Thailand. She longed for the day when she would be fluent in Thai, and to have God use her to draw others to Himself, even as He had done at home.

"Certainly within the next year I expect to see the results in my work among the Thai."

And during that year, the fledgling moved from Chainat to Hanka to try her wings.

Deep Waters

THE following summer Joan lay in bed in the mission hospital at Manorom. The stifling heat of the dry season weighed heavily on her as she dozed fitfully. The door quietly opened and Dorothy Mainhood, her old friend of camping days in the USA, hurried to the bedside.

"Swiftie, I just heard you were here."

She was shocked to see her friend looking so weak and thin.

Swiftie burst into tears. "Oh, Brownie, I thought you would never get back from your trip and that I would die before you came."

"Die? O Joanie, you *must* be ill! You didn't really think you were as bad as that, did you?"

"I was terribly ill at Hanka – much too ill really to travel. But I knew I had to get here, so I mustered all my strength and came. I hardly remember the first few days in bed, I was so ill. Now I'm feeling better but just so dreadfully weak."

"Why, I had no idea you were ill, Joan. But you mustn't be depressed. You'll soon be well again."

During the following weeks Dorothy spent as much as possible of her off-duty time with Joan, who was receiving the severe treatment for amoebic dysentery – a strength-sapping process. Daily Dorothy read the Bible to her and prayed with her. Joan was unusually quiet and subdued, but Dorothy attributed this to her illness.

Then the day came when Joan was well enough to leave the hospital. A little later she returned to Manorom to attend a friend's wedding and was delighted to see Dorothy again. One evening, as they were together, Dorothy thought how different Joan seemed – so terribly thin, almost bony. Her red hair, cut short because of the heat, was bleached from the sun. And she was so very quiet, not like her old self at all.

Suddenly Joan said, "Brownie, I've something to tell you. I have decided to ask the Hospital Superintendent about the advisability of my going home because of my health."

"Joan, you're not serious!"

"I'm very serious, Brownie. I just feel so useless here in Thailand. There's no point in my staying. I want to go home."

Dorothy could only stare at the once strong optimistic Joan, the one who had always been her tower of strength, her example of endurance and faith. Could this be Joan talking? It was unbelievable. She listened to her friend's story.

Day after day she had trudged the dusty, country roads around Hanka in the unbearable heat, carrying a load of books to sell. Her companion had been a senior missionary who spoke Thai fluently and who loved to be out preaching, teaching and witnessing. But with her limited Thai, Joan's main job was to sell books.

"Oh, I used all my charm to sell those books, so that the load would be lighter and I could catch a bus home. But how many times the last bus drove away just as I arrived. Oh, Brownie, I wouldn't mind the hard work and the heat and the choking thirst if only I felt I was accomplishing something. But it all seems so futile. At home God used me to lead others to Him. But here all I do is trudge around with everybody staring at my red hair and white skin! And I don't think I'll ever speak Thai well enough to help them really."

Dorothy sat stunned as the walls of comfort and courage that Joan had always been to her crumbled. Now it was her turn to be Joan's strength and comfort.

"But Joan," she began, "how can you say all your work has been useless? Our labour in the Lord is never in vain.

Remember that promise and all the others you used to quote to me -- the ones you used in camp-fire messages?"

"They can't have been meant for me," Joan said bitterly. "I've been claiming them, but they don't come true. I'm no help to my senior. I can feel my old stubbornness coming through and I know I'm a trial to her. I've tried to change but I can't!"

"Everything just looks dark to you now because you've been so ill. Depression often follows illness," Dorothy said. But the only reply was:

"I can hardly bear to think of camp at home and the happy, fruitful summers working with the girls there – oh, Dorothy, I *must* go home!"

Dorothy felt paralyzed as Joan went to find the doctor. With sinking heart she summoned every ounce of faith she had and cried desperately to God:

"Lord Jesus, keep her from any wrong action. Can it really be Your will that she should go home?"

Then Dorothy knew with a horrible certainty that Joan's desire to go home was not of God, but of the Evil One, and the thoughts she was entertaining were straight from him.

"O Lord, when Joan's friends prayed for her salvation years ago, You answered. Hear me now as You heard them then and save her from the deceptions of Satan."

For a long time Dorothy continued praying, unable to move from her seat, unaware of the gathering darkness. Finally the door opened. It was Joan.

"Dr. Chris [Maddox] wasn't in," she said quietly. "I didn't get to see him, so I've just been chatting."

A great weight lifted from Dorothy's heart. The two friends prayed together, and Joan never again mentioned the subject of going home and that very night asked God to give her the opportunity to start a girls' work in Thailand.

How had Joan reached such a low point? Obviously, it

did not happen overnight. It had begun at the start of her second year in the Far East when she had written to her Superintendent.

"Recent days have brought a heaviness within my heart. The novelty of things in general has begun to wear off. The drudgery of long hours in language study is exhausting. It is most frustrating when one longs to share the riches that we have in our Lord Jesus but lacks sufficient language."

Joan had claimed 2 Corinthians 6.16 during those days when she walked among the people but was unable to say much. "God hath said, I will dwell in them, and *walk* in them." Her prayer was that others might see Jesus in her as she walked among them.

In addition to the mental strain of language study, Joan had been troubled by illness. She, who had always enjoyed excellent health, wrote to Ruth in September, 1959. "For five months I have had amoebic cysts. It's quite a common complaint out here due to poor sanitation. Have been taking treatment for it, but can't get rid of them. Am getting nice and slim. I feel all right with the old stuff, but am sure it would be better without it."

In her prayer letter that autumn, Joan also revealed the struggle she was having with "self" as she tried to adjust to life in Thailand.

"I wanted to share my Beloved with those who have never met Him.
But, oh that language barrier.
I believe the work should be done 'thus'.
I believe converts should be trained 'thus'.
I don't like to study but I must spend six hours a day in the books.
I like to have my flower garden looking nice,
    but it is such a convenient place for the neighbours' rubbish – to say nothing of the plants that disappear.

I find it difficult to be constantly stared at,
   but is it any wonder when folk have only seen black
   hair and brown eyes.
I must decrease and He must increase."

Not only did Joan have to adjust to the Thai people
and their way of life; living with other missionaries also
demanded adjustments. An unmarried missionary does
not choose her co-worker and living companion. She may
find herself placed with someone of entirely different
temperament, background, interests, tastes and nation-
ality. Also, she may no sooner get accustomed to one place
and partner than she is moved to another centre. That
there are corners to be rubbed off and different ideas
about the best way to conduct the work is only natural,
but it takes supernatural grace and the power of God to
achieve harmony under these circumstances.

Joan was no exception to the rule, but here again she
was grateful for her college training and the lessons she
had learned in living with others and submitting to authority. Once, after helping herself to some jam a co-worker
had received from home, she was told she was incorrig-
ible! When she looked up the word in the dictionary she
was horrified to find the definition, "incapable of being
corrected, unreformable".

Joan was very critical of herself and felt sure at times
that she was a trial to her fellow workers. Yet their reports
to the Mission consistently described her as a cheerful,
co-operative worker, one whose sense of humour, friendly
helpfulness and unselfishness made her a joy to have around.

In December, 1958, Joan had been transferred to Hanka,
a small market town about six hours' journey down the
river from Chainat. There she and a senior worker, Joan
Wales, rented a room in a Thai home. The two Joans ate
in a local restaurant or sometimes made a simple meal
in their room, boiling water for tea on the family stove.

At first Swiftie had been thrilled at the opportunity to do pioneer work in the Hanka area, but her lack of facility in the language continued to hamper her. Once, when especially down-hearted, she shared her frustration with the other Joan – a small, energetic British woman who had done rugged pioneer work in China before coming to Thailand.

"If only I could speak Thai like you!" said Swiftie. "I long to start a work among Thai girls, but I'll never be able to do it if I can't get the language."

A verse which became especially meaningful to her at this time was Psalm 60.8, "Triumph thou because of me."

It was in Hanka that Swiftie contracted dysentery. The one room in the Thai house was an inconvenient place for Joan Wales to nurse her sick co-worker. Swiftie never grumbled or showed self-pity, but as soon as possible she went to the hospital in Manorom for proper treatment. It was there that she displayed the depths of discouragement which had so shocked Dorothy. Meanwhile Joan Wales had been transferred to Singapore, and since Swiftie could not remain alone in Hanka she returned to Chainat in June, 1959.

During these long months of illness and discouragement, Joan had not written home, and friends and relatives were much concerned. When at last she did write, she only hinted at what had taken place.

"Sometimes the Lord brings His children through very deep waters in order that they may be a little more conformed to His image. Yes, the waters have been very deep – so deep that letter writing was farthest from my heart. I needed the prayers of dear ones so very much. The battles in the 'deep waters' were both physical and spiritual, but praise the Lord with me, now I am feeling real good – in fact perfect. I'm returning to health even though thirty pounds lighter than when you last saw me. And the spiritual battles can best be summed up in the word 'victory' which is always ours if we persevere long enough, for we serve a risen, victorious Lord. How wonderful it was to prove Isaiah 43.2, 'When thou passest through the waters, I will be with thee'."

Only to her closest friends did Joan admit that she had been tempted to return home:

"I wish I could put down on paper what has been going on in this past year, but it just doesn't seem to come easily . . . . Believe me, more than once this wretch has wanted to be settled down at home, but His love and patience continued through it all."

The deep waters had been a time of humbling for Joan – a time when she had become painfully aware of her own inadequacy – physically, mentally and spiritually. She knew now as never before the reality of Christ's words, "Without me, ye can do nothing."

Back with Grace Harris in Chainat, Joan, now making encouraging progress in the language, looked forward to working with the children in a more active way than before. But on the second day there she received a letter from the Acting Field Superintendent, Mr. Frey, which made her mouth fall open as she read it.

"Listen to this! Mr. Frey wants me to consider going to Saraburi with Rosa Brand. I would have to act as the senior missionary because I've been in Thailand longer than Rosa. Can you imagine me a senior missionary? Why, I haven't even been here two years yet myself. But Mr. Frey says there's no one else to go."

"Well, Joan, that sounds like a fine opportunity," her friend replied.

"But all that responsibility! Why, I thought only second-term missionaries have charge of centres. The Mission must be falling to pieces if they don't have anyone more qualified than I am."

But as Joan prayed about it, she recognized God's hand in opening this door. The deep waters had been for a purpose, God was preparing her for a larger task. And so once again she got out her boxes and trunks and began to pack.

In her next prayer letter, Joan quoted Psalm 66.12, "We went through fire and through water: but thou broughtest us out into a wealthy place." The "wealthy place" was Saraburi – wealthy in opportunity for God.

A Wealthy Place

JOAN slept little her first night in Saraburi. The oppressive heat and the noises of her new surroundings made her restless. Sudden loud shouts jolted her out of her drowsy state. The neighbours were quarrelling. She heard pounding and screaming. The husband must have come home drunk and was beating his children. Joan and Rosa had been warned about this. "If only I could help those poor little ones," thought Joan.

Although it was past midnight the noise of the traffic was still loud, the mission house being very close to the main road. By day, noise from the passing vehicles often drowned conversation, and the buses threw up clouds of dust and dirt. This and a boys' school next door allowed little quiet or privacy. Passers-by often stood and stared in at the front door. Some used the alley outside the kitchen window for a toilet. Robbery was always a danger to be guarded against.

"O dear God, why did You send me to take charge of such a place?" Joan prayed one night. Then she recalled the words of Scripture, "Is anything too hard for the Lord? . . . With God all things are possible." Comforted, she drifted off to sleep.

Although "wealthy" in opportunity, Joan's new field did not look very promising for the Gospel. Saraburi is a Buddhist "Mecca" famous for the Footprint of Buddha, supposedly proving that Buddha had walked here. Special festivals are celebrated each year commemorating the time when the footprint was discovered. Although there are many reputed footprints in Asia, only two are officially recognized – this one in Saraburi and one in Ceylon. The so-called footprint is an oval depression about a yard long and a foot deep and bears little resemblance to a human foot. A shrine has been built over it, guarded by twenty hideous images, their heads hooded and having ivory teeth, red eyes and distended nostrils. Here, too, stands a chapel devoted to the fierce god of death. Saraburi has been described as a "grossly idolatrous town, which the Thai would like to make a centre of pilgrimage for Buddhists all over the world", and "an unfruitful place to witness".

Into this centre of Buddhism and idolatry the two inexperienced young missionaries, Joan and her Swiss partner, Rosa, moved. Rosa was a tall, slim blonde of a more serious nature than Joan. Both were hard workers.

Surprisingly, it was in this "unfruitful place" that Joan's work in Thailand first bore tangible fruit. She reported:

"It has now pleased the Lord to allow me to see my first Thai come to Him. He is Puan, a young soldier, who has been studying English with me. On our field many have professed to become Christians, but very few seem to go on. The pressure from the Evil One is terrific and they just give up. The Thai temperament is so carefree and nonchalant that it carries over into their Christian life. Oh, that Puan may be a good soldier for the Lord and that the church here in Saraburi may be built upon the Christ in his life! Until last week our Sunday service consisted of us two and that's all. Last week Puan came. What a thrill to have someone with whom to share the Word!"

The work at Saraburi was varied; children's meetings, Sunday Schools, English Bible classes, and leprosy work which Joan described in a letter:

"Our leprosy work is increasing and we now have ninety patients registered. They come for their medicine just once a month, so we try to visit their homes to follow up the contact with them. This gives a wonderful opportunity to show the love of God because these dear people are so rejected by man. The Lord is certainly fulfilling His promise of rewarding our labour as we see Mrs. Neuay, the one leprosy Christian, growing in the Lord. We go out to her house once a week for Bible study.

"I'm having a really good opportunity with twenty teenage girls who come to study English, using the Bible. Would love you to remember these girls, that the Word of God may fall on good ground. I also have a class of eighteen boys and girls in their late teens who come for English. One of my favourite times of the week is what I call my Pioneer Girls' group. Seven of these girls have made a profession of faith, but two have moved away and three don't come any longer. Yet the Lord has promised to keep His own. The other two are very faithful in coming. Please pray that they will grow up in Him. Their names are Pen-see and Dook-ah-da. Also, remember those who are not yet His.

"I have been much concerned about reaching the young boys in our neighbourhood. These boys are too old for our Sunday School, so I have started a club for them and am teaching them baseball. They think it great fun to play this foreign game – so do I! The greatest joy is to see them gather around the Word for a time of study before we play. Oh, that many of these may really become flames of fire for the Lord!"

Joan was greatly relieved when in February, 1960, May Campbell, an experienced worker, came to head up the work in Saraburi. Now there were two Irish redheads in Saraburi, for May, too, had auburn hair and came from the land of Joan's forbears, Ireland.

"I've laughed more since her arrival than I have for months," wrote Joan. "That good old Irish wit is great to have around. I wish you could hear what has happened to my New England accent, between studying Thai and living with a gal from Ireland and another from Switzerland."

Joan remained at Saraburi for more than two years. There her vision for youth work grew, as daily she watched hundreds of Thai students pass the mission house on their way to school. Often she said to May, "I dream of the day when scores of these young people will gather together to sing praises to the Lord and to study His Word."

But Joan did more than dream. She visited nearby homes and invited the teenagers in. She always prepared carefully for their coming and planned an interesting programme for them. Many times May found her "sitting on the floor, Thai-style, with teenagers all around her playing games, studying the Bible, or eating home-made Thai sweets". Joan did not spare herself in her effort to love and win these young people, and several did come to trust the Saviour.

There was one girl in whom Joan took a special interest. The girl helped her mother make a living by selling sweets on the roadside near the mission home. Often on the day of the meeting, Joan went along with her to help her sell by urging people to buy, demonstrating how good they were by eating some herself, and buying more to bring home. Thus, the girl was able to finish early and come to the meeting.

In one area where Joan and May held a children's

D

meeting, the youngsters were so rowdy and disobed-
ient that the missionaries could hardly hear themselves
talk. One day the children and May were left standing,
gaping, as Joan suddenly announced:

"There will be no story today."

Gathering up her books and flannelgraph materials,
she walked off home. May could do nothing but close
the meeting, telling the children they must behave or
there would be no more meetings. As a result their behaviour improved, for they knew the missionaries meant
what they said.

Joan was delighted to be chosen to serve on the OMF
Youth Committee for Central Thailand. In this capacity
during her last year before furlough, she travelled around
to conduct special youth days on many different stations.
She described one of these visits in a letter.

" 'By Camp Cherith's shining waters . . . ' Oh no, I
mean by Thailand's muddy waters . . . As I sat on the
shore early in the morning watching the water flow by
and the people come and go in their little boats en route
to market, I realized that whether it is at Camp Cherith or
here in this little village, my purpose is still the same –
that of proclaiming the unsearchable riches of Christ.
Oh, that these people who use the waterways so freely
for every purpose – bathing, dish-washing, laundry, transportation – would only come to know the Giver of every
good and perfect gift! But no, it is the goddess of the
water that receives their appreciation, if they give thanks
at all.

"My heart turned from prayer for the multitudes to
praise for the one and only Christian woman in that area,
Mrs. O, the one in whose home we were to spend the
next three days. My fellow worker and I had come to
hold children's meetings, but of course our days were
filled with many other things as well.

"I was thankful that I had lived in this land long enough

not to let the many pairs of brown eyes staring at us from daybreak till darkness bother me. Of course, to those in the household, it was probably one of the most exciting things that had ever happened – the foreign teachers coming to live with them. We heard all about the preparations that had preceded us from the four-year-old son named 'Little'. First of all he informed us that the mosquito net and bedding were all new, not what his father used when he came home from his gambling den once a month. 'Little' also told us just what space on the floor would be our sleeping quarters. The first area was for him, baby sister, his seven-year-old sister, and mother. The second sleeping net housed two older brothers, and the third net was for the foreign teachers. The house consisted of only one room, so once again I was thankful for the little I had learned regarding Thai ways, especially their custom of bathing in a *pa* and getting into clean clothing under the same *pa*. This *pa* is a piece of cloth that is worn as a *sarong*, but when bathing it is tied up around one's chest and reaches to the knees. Believe me, it is quite an art to keep decent throughout this procedure, and all those big brown eyes peeping around the corners were probably suprised to see the foreigners carrying on in Thai fashion. 'Little' also informed us that the hot sauce on our rice had been made from a chicken he had had since it was just a chick. He seemed rather proud that he was willing to have it killed and eaten by us, but I must confess, I wasn't too eager to eat any more after I heard his little story.

"The opportunities of Bible study and prayer with 'Mother' were one of the highlights of the time. Mrs. O was baptized at Easter and has really been going on with the Lord. She has a very quiet way about her and yet seems to have a consistent testimony before her friends and neighbours. It was interesting to note her concern for the salvation of those to whom she had been witness-

ing. One morning my fellow-worker prayed for those to
whom Mrs. O witnessed. She just used the term 'the
ladies' but Mrs. O chimed right in and mentioned each one
by name. Such a perfect example of a child coming to
a father!

"Speaking of praying, I dropped a brick! I wanted to
ask the Lord to make Mrs. O a good witness, but because
I used the wrong Thai word, I asked Him to make her a
good worm. Oh well, maybe she'll think I was referring
to Psalm 22 where the Psalmist cried, 'I am a worm . . . '

"After our times of devotion with Mrs. O, we went
out to the market to talk with different ones. Then in the
afternoon after school we had our meetings. The children
attended the temple school, and in the four years I have
been in Thailand I have never seen such opposition. The
teachers forbade the children to come; they were made
to form a line and walk past the house where we were
having the meetings. When they reached the market,
they could break line and go home, but praise the Lord,
many of them just turned around and came back to the
meeting. The first day, in the middle of the story, someone
yelled,

" 'The teacher is coming!'

"The children of his class jumped up and ran to hide
until he was past. They said he would penalize any he
saw at the meeting.

"Many were hindered from coming because of this,
but those who did come heard about the one and only
true God who loves each one of them. Their memory
verse was, 'Thou shalt have no other gods before me.
Thou shalt not make unto thee any graven image . . . .
Thou shalt not bow down thyself to them, nor serve
them . . . ' This cuts right across the core of life in this
land of Buddhism. Is it any wonder the Evil One roars
about, seeking whom he may devour?

" 'For we wrestle not against flesh and blood, but

against principalities, against powers, against the rulers of the darkness of this world, against spiritual wickedness in high places' (Ephes. 6.12).

"The usual comment in this land when one presents the Gospel is, 'Oh, it's the same as Buddhism!' Now the comments in the market are, 'Why do the teachers forbid the children to go to the meetings if it's the same?' This gives us an opportunity to explain the difference.

"The evenings are spent helping the older students with English. The first night we used the story of Creation, and I asked them if they ever thanked God for the water He gives them and for all the fish in their waterways. One student answered, 'We never knew whom to thank'. Could it be that there will be those along that river who will no longer worship the goddess of the water but the Creator Himself?"

The more Joan worked with Thai children and youth, the more she longed to start a programme similar to Pioneer Girls and Christian Service Brigade. This burden she shared with Pioneer Girls' staff members:

"I have just come in from playing basketball with a group of boys. I live right next door to a gambling alley, and these boys gamble all day long during their holidays. They are much upon my heart.

"The Lord has seen fit to put me on a new committee here in Thailand for work among children and youth. You can imagine how my heart aches as I look out on the thousands of Thai kids and realize that three others and I now shoulder the responsibility of reaching them. To some degree it's as you look out upon your mission field of girls. At any rate, you are able to pray intelligently regarding this burden, and I would tell you, dear ones, that if the Lord has chosen this child of His to give her life for the kids in Thailand to become His, then I long with every ounce of strength to give myself for this cause."

Furlough time neared, and Joan began preparations to

go home and report to her young supporters, now 60,000 strong. She wanted to share with them her concern for the Thai youth and urge them to pray for Thailand – that in this land so wealthy in opportunities to sow God's Word, there might be a rich harvest of young people who love and serve Jesus Christ.

In the autumn of 1961 Joan left Thailand for furlough in the United States with the prayer upon her heart that God might use her when she returned to found a work among Thai youth.

One Hundred and Thirty-four Beds

THE phone rang in the Bible Institute at Seeheim, Germany. A secretary answered. "Guten Tag. Bibel-schule Bergstrasse."

"May I speak to Ginny Anderson, please?" said the voice at the other end.

Ginny hurried to the phone. "Hullo, is that Joanie? Where are you? Ginny Enck and I waited hours for you this morning at the Darmstadt railway station. We finally gave up and came home."

"I'm sorry. We left Switzerland later than we had planned. We're at the Post Office across from the station. There's no currency exchange here and we had no German money for a phone call. But I found a man here in the Post Office who speaks English and he lent me money to call you. We have to wait right here until you come and pay him for the call."

"We'll be there in twenty minutes."

"Typical Joanie!" said Ginny laughing, as she and the other Ginny sped to Darmstadt in the little black Volkswagen. "The last time she came through Germany I lived in Heidelberg. That time she got off at the wrong stop, so when she came in later on a different platform I missed her. I was frantic, hunting all over the station. Finally, I drove home, only to find her climbing out of a taxi in front of the house. I'm for ever meeting people at airports and railway stations and never have any trouble except when Joanie arrives."

Joan's furlough had begun. Through the generosity of a missionary friend from Australia, she was her companion on a tour of Italy and Switzerland. The tour over, Joan's friend headed for her home in Australia, while Joan stayed on on the Continent for ten days with two friends from camp and college days, both of whom now worked at the German Bible Institute.

During her brief stay Joan visited German homes and spoke through interpretation at various meetings for children, youth and adults. Although she could not understand German she enjoyed getting to know German believers at the Bible Institute and in the homes and groups she visited. The three friends had much to share. During a drive through the lovely mountains of the Black Forest Joan spoke of some of the "deep water" experiences in Thailand.

"Had not so many miles of ocean separated me from home I might have given up and left," she confessed, "But missionary work was never easy. When you work in territory which Satan has controlled for centuries, there is certain to be opposition. Only in the power of God is there any possibility of success."

The time in Germany went by all too quickly before Joan boarded the train for England. After a short visit to friends there she sailed for New York.

"The skyline of New York," she wrote, "came into view and excitement climbed higher and higher – first the Statue of Liberty, and then the American flag flying, until at last I was standing on American soil surrounded by loved ones. The thrilling hour of being whisked home came, and my, how bright those New York lights are, how long the cars, and how fast everyone was moving! Would we get home safely? How thankful I was that the answer was 'Yes' – safe and sound, to spend the next few weeks getting to know my nieces and nephews again, for there had been many changes in the past five years. Not only was it wonderful to be home, but it was Christmas time – a time that isn't celebrated in Thailand, where so few know the Christ of Christmas."

After the holidays, Swiftie began many months of travelling – visiting Pioneer Girls' clubs all over the United States and Canada, and by her own count, sleeping in one hundred and thirty-four beds.

Swiftie prayed much that God would give her a message for furlough. She had also spent much time preparing. To illustrate a typical day in the life of a Thai girl she had brought Thai clothing, a model of a Thai home, pictures and many other items. Everywhere she spoke, her presentation of missions was well received. The youngest Pilgrim could understand it, and yet it had meaning for the high school Explorer as well. People marvelled at Joan's ability to organize and conduct large rallies for the Pioneer Girls, complete with Thai games, singing and an illustrated talk. And Swiftie herself found it exhilarating to be speaking again in her native tongue.

"I'm loving it," she wrote, "and yet deep within I'm longing to see an everlasting work of the Spirit of God in our midst at every meeting."

One of the high points of Joan's travels was speaking at an Explorer leadership conference on the West Coast. Several years later, one of the girls present wrote:

"I will always remember the night of the worship service. The Lord seemed so close to everyone, and I remember looking at Swiftie and seeing the loveliness of Christ through her. When I think of Swiftie, I think of the word 'sparkle'. She did shine. When she gave her testimony, I realized that Christ did not have full control of my life. So I gave my life to Him and I'm willing to do whatever He wants me to do."

Swiftie was very enthusiastic about Pioneer Girls' new magazine *Trails*. In her meetings she distributed special subscription order blanks and promised to send a small gift from Thailand to every girl who ordered one subscription for herself and got one other girl to subscribe. When these order blanks arrived at the Pioneer Girls' office, names and addresses were relayed to Swiftie. By the time she returned to Thailand, she had a long list of names. To each one she sent a picture postcard and a Thai coin with the king's profile on it. On the card she wrote:

If your *Trails* re-subscription has come due
Hope this little gift will remind you to renew.

Across the miles it comes your way,
To find a place with you to stay.

On your dressing table it will do
As a reminder that "I love you".

And I hope the coin you see
Will remind you to pray for me.

Swiftie

God's hand was over Swiftie throughout her months of travel. Once while staying with Dorothy Mainhood's parents near Coleman, Michigan, she was due to drive to an evening meeting in Bay City, thirty-six miles away.

It began to snow during the day and by late afternoon had turned into a real blizzard.

"Do you think you should go?" asked Mrs. Mainhood anxiously. "The snow is drifting badly and the roads may be impassable by the time you return."

"The Lord took care of me in Thailand and He can do it in Michigan, too," was Joan's reply.

Mrs. Mainhood gave her a pair of woollen slacks, a scarf and high boots to take along in case she got stranded. Then the family waited for her, praying for her safe return. Shortly after 11 p.m. they heard what sounded like a car and hurried to the window, expecting to see Swiftie's car. Instead, they saw a snow plough drive in and Swiftie alighting from the cab! How relieved they were!

"The car stalled a few miles down the road and I started to walk," she told them. "I had to wade through drifts above my knees and was getting exhausted when suddenly a snow plough came along and picked me up."

Swiftie had no car of her own. Anticipating much travelling during the summer, she began to ask God for the use of a Rambler with seats which could be made into a bed. One day, a Pioneer Girls' staff member was talking to a friend who said:

"I won't need my car if I go to camp this summer and just wish I knew of someone who could use it. I would rather have it in use than standing idle."

The staff member told her that Joan was praying for a car. And the car in question was a Rambler with the type of seats Joan wanted!

But even Swiftie did not escape the difficulty that most missionaries have in readjusting to the home country after a term on the field. Her years of "identifying" with the people of her adopted land could not be shed overnight and she felt a bit strange and uncertain the first few weeks and months at home. Writing to Cyril Faulkner in Thailand she said,

"These are certainly difficult days. I believe the change is good, and yet, honestly, I feel very much like a fish out of water. Have tried real hard to get wrapped up in Pioneer Girls again, but don't seem to be able to. Am wondering if I lost something of this as I endeavoured to become identified with our Thai friends. I look forward to my return ever so much – and for this, I thank Him."

However, as the months went by, Joan readjusted to American life, renewed old friendships and made new ones. When the time to return to the field drew near, she had mixed emotions, wanting to get back to the land to which God had called her and yet reluctant to break ties with friends and family at home again.

Sometimes while travelling alone on long trips, Joan thought about all that lay before her in Thailand. She no longer had any illusions about the romance of missionary work. Everywhere she went people said, "The political situation looks black in the Far East. Aren't you afraid to return?"

In May, fear that the Communist forces in Laos might move across the border into Thailand brought 4,000 American troops plus troops from other SEATO nations into Thailand.

"And what about your health?" friends asked. It was true that Joan would never be free of the amoebic cysts; they might reactivate at any time should she get run down physically.

But these were not the things which bothered Joan most. She feared more the spiritual battles in Thailand where the work was often discouraging and results were meagre. Joan sensed, too, that one cause of her reluctance to return was her ego. In America she enjoyed the prestige of a missionary. She was admired, she was the centre of attention wherever she spoke, gifts were lavished upon her and people responded to her message. In Thailand she would again be a 'nobody'.

Then, too, Joan received a letter in March which brought her keen disappointment. Believing that her desire to start a youth work in Thailand was God-given, she had requested to be assigned to this work full-time upon her return. But she read:

"The Field Council has not felt led to assign you to full-time youth work for the present, though we are hoping to place you in a centre where it will be possible to have a group of girls and possibly a group of boys, too, to show what can be done in this type of work."

There was one other major concern that caused Joan to consider seriously postponing her return to Thailand. During her travels she had noticed that many girls gave regularly to missions, but had little understanding of the Biblical basis for missions. This led her to feel that there was need for better missionary education material for club leaders and she wondered if perhaps she could request an extension of her furlough to work on such a project.

This concern was expressed in a letter to a Pioneer Girls' board member.

"God has given me a dual ministry; one in Thailand and the other with Pioneer Girls. I have become even more conscious of this recently – indeed He has given me a unique opportunity with girls and guides – a responsibility that cannot be lightly overlooked. The demands in Thailand are great, the labourers are few, the night cometh, and God has recommissioned this child of His to return; at the same time He has burdened me regarding the need in our missionary programme. His purpose for this is yet veiled, for reasons beyond my understanding, and yet, how it crowds me to Him in order to know His will. 'Ready to go, ready to stay, ready to do Thy will.' If He reveals to all concerned that this is the time and that there may be some way in which I could help, then may His will be done.

"I do believe that one of the main reasons God has blessed and increased our organization is that, as we have been "looking unto Jesus", we have seen His vision not only of those at our doorstep but those in the regions beyond. This vision must be imparted to those He has entrusted to us. I realize there are many other needs demanding attention and yet I'm sure you would agree that this which is the heart-throb of our Lord is vital."

In the end, it was agreed that Joan should return on schedule and that others on the Pioneer Girls' staff would work on the missionary education materials.

Wherever she travelled, Joan left one impression – her love for people and for the Lord, and her zest for life. People commented frequently on this – her fun, her interest in people, her natural down-to-earth spirituality, her sincerity and her humility.

People noticed, too, Joan's unusual love for children and their spontaneous response to her. No matter how busy her schedule in Thailand or on furlough, she always found time to do special things with the children who crossed her path. She would take them to a playground or a beach, or plan a little party for them with decorations and favours. Instinctively she understood the needs and interest of a child, and her creative imagination never failed to fascinate them. A missionary couple in Thailand gave an example of this.

"It was our joy to spend part of our vacation with Joanie at the mission vacation home, Pinecrest, in Chiengmai. She was so kind and thoughtful with the children, buying them gifts in Bangkok and bringing them with her to Pinecrest. She made up a game by hiding the gifts in the garden, and then had the children go out to find them. They were thrilled! Lenny, our eldest, loved her and enjoyed sitting on her lap and playing with her."

Joan decided to use some personal gifts of money to buy something representing a child – a figurine or painting – to take back to Thailand with her. She and a friend spent many hours in Chicago looking through stores and galleries, but never found just the right thing at the right price. Finally, the art editor of *Trails* magazine made a painting from a photograph of a Thai girl about ten years of age. Joan was delighted to have this picture to hang in her room.

One of the last things Joan did before returning to Thailand was to look up her mother. It took a long day of searching, for she had moved, but Joan finally found her. The visit, however, was a disappointment. A few days later, she spoke at Maine Camp Cherith on Psalm 27.10, "When my father and my mother forsake me, then the Lord will take me up."

"I know now that the Lord Himself is enough – and that He alone can truly satisfy."

Joan's furlough ended in late September, 1962. On her last afternoon in America she sat in the home of a friend in Seattle, Washington, listening to records of her favourite music from Handel's *"Messiah"*. In a few hours she was to board a jet and head west out over the Pacific toward the Far East. Parting from close friends and family was harder this time than the last. Joan's second term seemed to stretch out endlessly before her – four long years filled with the unknown. Would she again face deep waters – illness, discouragements, homesickness?

Again and again Joan played the aria, "He shall feed His flock like a shepherd, and He shall gather the lambs with His arm, . . . and carry them in His bosom, and gently lead those that are with young." How comforting to know that this kind Shepherd was her Shepherd, that He would go before her to prepare the way! Following Him, she need have no fears.

Friendship Club

ONCE Joan was under way, her attitude began to change to one of keen anticipation. She made one stop in Hawaii and another in Japan. The closer Joan got to Thailand, the more eager she was to see her friends there and to take up her work again.

Upon arrival in the autumn of 1962, Joan was again assigned to Paknampho, the largest city in Central Thailand with a population of 30,000. Located at the junction of three rivers, the city is an important centre of commerce and transportation. The OMF house is in the south end of the city just behind a Caltex station, and over the gateway between high, white walls hangs a welcome sign reading in Thai, "The house that teaches the Christian religion. We are happy to receive anyone seeking the truth." The words are especially appropriate in a Buddhist land, for Buddha's advice to his disciples was, "Seek the truth".

Ruby Lundgren and Mary Cooke gave Joan a warm welcome. Her coming was an answer to prayer, for one of their goals was to have youth work established in Paknampho by 1965, the 100th anniversary of the Mission. Joan's coming brought this goal within sight.

"The Lord gave great joy in returning," wrote Joan in her first letter to friends at home. "The language has come back rather quickly, the only trouble is, I didn't have much language to lose in the first place! Am asking the Lord to give me good language in order that the people may find it easier to listen to me. Readjustment is fairly easy – weather and food no problem. Customs are a bit different – am having to learn all over again that I need a heart of love. Am finding the sin of selfishness cropping up all the time, as well as other sins I thought were once and for all conquered. I guess there isn't any such thing as once for all; but for the grace of God, one falls in a moment."

Joan's living conditions were quite different from those during the latter part of her first term when she had worked in more remote and primitive districts.

"Paknampho is quite an up and coming city with many modern conveniences, such as running water and electricity. We even have a local bus service, and when we go to the market now we get our food in plastic bags instead of wrapped up in a banana leaf. We have a hairdresser's near our house and it's great to be able to have one's hair done for the exorbitant price of five cents! Every time I go I think of furlough days, when a trip to the hairdresser's cost me two dollars fifty cents. It makes me enjoy my five cents' worth. We live in a big house. It has to be big for eight of us! Ruby Lundgren, who had thirty-one years in China, is my senior worker. She's sixty-seven now and should have retired, but presses faithfully on, putting many of us new workers to shame with what she accomplishes from day to day. When new workers come to Thailand, many come to Paknampho for language study, and so we have many comings and goings."

The work in Paknampho was similar to that of Joan's former centre; Sunday Schools, children's meetings, English classes for teenagers, services with the few Christians. There were also special events such as Christmas programmes, evangelistic campaigns and Sunday School rallies.

Joan at once started a club for boys and one for girls. The girls, especially, were responsive and three older ones became believers; Golden Needle, Sugarcane and Wantani.

Just as Joan began to settle down in the work at Paknampho, an interruption came. The Sunday morning before Christmas Joan was reading the Christmas story in Thai when the words of Mary to the angel arrested her attention. "Behold the handmaid of the Lord; be it unto me according to thy word." In Thai the word for "hand-maid" is translated "bondslave", and Joan pondered the significance for herself.

"O Lord Jesus," she prayed, "I truly want to be your bondslave at any cost. These may be dangerous words to tell You because You may ask me to do something that will cost me a lot, yet with all my heart I mean these words. I am Your bondslave, ready to do whatever You ask."

That afternoon a telegram arrived for Joan asking her to go to Saraburi, her old centre, temporarily to replace a worker who had had to leave suddenly on account of illness.

"How *can* I leave Paknampho now – just when I've got settled and started my clubs? And what about the three girls who have just become believers? I *must* stay and teach them how to live as Christians."

But even as these objections arose in her mind, the words she had read that morning stood out above all else – "bondslave of the Lord". Quietly she prayed, "Thank You, Lord Jesus, for preparing my heart this morning. How can I help but love You? Yes, I *am* Your bondslave and I *will* obey you. I will go to Saraburi trusting You to care for these girls, for they belong to You."

Before she left, Joan turned over to the other missionaries her well-prepared plans so that they could carry on the clubs until she returned.

Joan always made it a practice to choose a Scripture verse at the beginning of each new year to be her verse for the year. As 1963 opened she shared her verses in a letter to a friend.

"The Lord's Word to me regarding 1963 comes from Luke 10.42 and 39. One thing is needful . . . sit at Jesus' feet, and hear His word. How much I feel I need this! I get so wrapped up in the work and yet all the time I know very well that the real value is in that time alone with Him. Am asking Him to teach me to really meet

with Him during prayer. How I long to really know Him!
I don't feel I'm getting to know Him more and more as
the years go on. In fact, I find myself not as in love with Him
after ten years as I was after five. Feel that I must lay
everything aside to return to my first love. Revelation
2.2-4 is so true:

" 'I know your industry and activities, laborious toil
and trouble, . . . I know you are enduring patiently and
are bearing up for My name's sake, and you have not
fainted or become exhausted or grown weary. But I have
this against you, that you have left the love that you had
at first – you have deserted Me, your first love.'[1]

"Oh, may He have mercy on all who profess to be His
and in a like state!"

Joan could never put out of her mind her concern to
start a Christian youth work. On January 15 she wrote:

"My heart cries out for the intermediate age group of
this land. There is hardly anything being done for them,
and everyone is up to his ears in work; no one can possibly
take on anything else. The labourers are few, nevertheless
the God-given burden cannot be cast off. I have just
returned from a youth committee meeting where once
again I presented a paper on this and shared my burden
for reaching the young people with an organized programme
instead of this 'hit and miss' business. I believe our days
are few here in this country, and if we don't meet the
needs of these young people now, the opportunity will be
lost. All on the committee were of one accord, but the
Field Council must approve it. Please pray with me that
if this programme is the Lord's choice for Thailand, I'll
be given the 'go ahead' on it."

Joan had to wait several months before the Field Council
met again. When at last it did, her request was approved.

---

[1] *The Amplified New Testament,* Marshall, Morgan & Scott Ltd.,
London.

After her return to Paknampho from Saraburi, she wrote home joyfully:

"Hi! Have some wonderful news for you. (No, I'm not getting married – sorry!) But the time has come for me to work on adapting Pioneer Girls to Thai culture – am I ever excited? Have plunged in full steam ahead. The Mission has asked me to adapt it for both boys and girls."

At first Joan hoped to have the materials ready for the following year, but it soon became evident that this was a much bigger task than she had anticipated. She began by studying all the existing youth programmes in Thailand, both secular and Christian. As she pored over the Pioneer Girls' material, she realized that much adaptation would be necessary if the programme was to fit the Thai culture. The name and theme and much of the badge work were inappropriate. Yet she was convinced that Thai girls would respond to a programme with the same underlying principles as Pioneer Girls. Thai girls, too, needed a Christ-centred club related to the local church. They needed contact with a leader who was a woman of God. They needed to learn to study the Bible for themselves and to take Christ into every phase of their lives. And they needed training in order to serve and lead in the young Thai church. These were the principles Joan sought to incorporate as she planned an achievement programme to help girls measure steps of progress in Bible study and in learning useful skills for home and community.

It took many months before Joan hit on an appropriate theme. Her first thought was a royal theme, for Christian girls are daughters of the King of kings. But Thai people assured her that in a land where the king is held in such high esteem, a royal theme would be improper for her club. Finally a Thai Christian girl suggested the friendship theme, and this appealed to Joan.

Meanwhile Joan took her share in the general work at the centre and continued language study. Because she did not excel in the language, she had to spend many hours of preparation whenever she had to speak at a meeting. She could never speak at short notice therefore, but when she did speak, she did very well. She took regular lessons from a tutor who helped her put her messages into good Thai and recorded them on tape. Joan listened to the tape over and over again, in order to get the pronunciation and sentence construction firmly in mind. Before 1963 was over, she had passed her fifth and last language exam.

Ruby Lundgren appreciated Joan's contribution to the centre. "She brightened and enlivened the scene with her cheerful presence and radiant personality. The Thai loved her for her happy spirit. She always did more than her share of the practical work. She was handy with the saw and hammer and, when any jobs needed doing, she was the one to whom we turned."

Once the missionaries wanted to have a booth at a fair which would represent the three categories of Christian work being done in Thailand: medical, educational and church work. Joan made a large map from plywood, showing the locations of the work, and equipped it with electric lights and a push button, so that the church work was shown by a green light, the school work by blue, and the medical work by red. This ingenious device attracted many to the booth where they received Gospel literature and a word of personal testimony.

Because of Joan's talents at carpentry, the Thai sometimes called her *Naichang* (carpenter). One evening Joan climbed a tree and sawed off a branch that was shutting out the light from Mary Cooke's room. When the washing girl saw the branch the next morning she asked who had cut it off. The cook replied:

"*Naichang*, of course; who do you think?"

Mary Cooke admired Joan's self discipline and organizational ability. "I have never before or since lived such an organized life in the centre as I did when Joan was there," she said later. "Everything Joan had a part in had to be well prepared in advance. When we had our Christmas programmes for the various age divisions, Joan had everything thoroughly planned and organized from the decorations and refreshments right down to the last detail of the programme. The result was the most effective and smoothest series we had ever had."

The months went by and still the Friendship Club programme was not ready. From the beginning Joan prayed for Thai co-workers. She knew two women who were possibilities. Great was her heartache when her high hopes for them were dashed. One had an illegitimate child, and the other stabbed and wounded a woman whom her husband had brought into the home as a second wife. Though both repented and Joan continued to befriend them, she knew she could not use them in her new work.

During these discouraging days, Joan wrote:

"It takes every bit of God-given grace and faith to live victoriously out here. It's a constant battle – can't ease up for a second, really one can't. These are hard days with nothing to encourage – a handful of Christians, none completely His. The situation is driving me to Him, my only Hope. He has to be my vision moment by moment. Does the Pioneer Girls' motto 'Looking unto Jesus' mean anything to this child of His? Guess you know it does. Only the grace of God keeps me pressing on, constantly I hear Him say, 'My child, what is that to thee? Follow thou Me.' Then I look away to Him."

Joan revealed her great concern for those without Christ in a letter to an old friend from Pioneer Girls camp.

"It is at this point that pain comes within my heart. I know there are endless needs at home for real women of God, but oh, dear Penny, if one could but see the situation here in the East, and the tremendous need for someone to come and help give the Bread of Life to the

millions who have never even heard His precious name
once! Sorry, Penny, I'm getting off on to something that
lies deep within my soul and I can't mention it too often.
Thanks for listening."

Nor could Joan ignore the needs of those around her
during the months of working on her future programme.
In December she wrote:

"These days have brought a burning within my soul to
preach the unsearchable riches of Christ. The Lord has
shown me a way whereby I may unburden my soul. I am
memorizing five messages that I hope to give on five
consecutive nights in one area and then move on to repeat
them in another area. Here in this province there are
600,000 people, most of whom have not yet heard, so the
sowing must be done in order to have the golden harvest.
Please pray that the message will go forth in the power of
the Holy Spirit."

Before Joan could carry out these plans, the youth
committee asked her to put aside all other work and
concentrate on the materials for the Club programme.
In March, 1964, she wrote, "It's such a big job – even
overwhelming. But I've prayed for many years that the
Lord would give me a job to do for Himself and He has
answered."

By August, when the material was ready for the final
touches and translation into Thai, Joan moved to Bangkok
to work with a Thai Christian, Mrs. Jitbanjong, for several
weeks. Finally, when the material was ready to go to the
printers, Joan returned to Paknampho.

On October 2 Joan decided to write to friends at home
But first her plants had to be watered and her furniture
dusted. Her room was cosy, attractive and always neat.
Some of the furniture she had made herself – the clothes
cupboard, book case and cabinet. To make the cabinet
she had taken an old orange crate, added shelves and a

door, and painted it green. From an old hurricane lamp, Joan had made an electric lamp, using a Thai farmer's hat as a lampshade. Interesting knick-knacks and several plants were scattered about the room, including the inevitable piece of driftwood, set in a pot with ivy climbing over it. Two paintings of Thai girls hung on the wall, one made by Joan's friend in America and another which she had found in Chiengmai.

Eventually Joan sat down at her typewriter. She began her letter with a poem of A. A. Milne, adapting it to herself ("mish" was her abbreviation for missionary).

> There was an old "mish" you once knew,
> Who had so many things she'd to do
> That whenever she thought it was time to begin
> She couldn't because of the state she was in.
> (Guess who???)

"Why, oh, why does Swiftie find it so hard to write? Well, even now as she starts this letter she finds herself in quite a state of turmoil trying to decide which she should do: her own personal Bible study, her Thai Bible study, language study, preparation for her Sunday School, sorting Bible study material for Club work, or write a letter. Now, as you well know, that which she feels has the lowest priority is the letter, and yet today she is down to this job because she needs pen pals for some of her girls. They are very excited about this, so I would appreciate your help if you know of any girls around twelve to fourteen years of age who would enjoy having a Thai pen pal. Thanks very much!

"Well, what in the world does ol' Swiftie-bird do out there in Thailand anyway? Most of my time recently has been spent on adapting the Pioneer Girls' programme to Thai culture – a much bigger job than I had anticipated, but praise the Lord, it has been completed. The name of the Club is the Friendship Club. The motto is 'A friend loveth at all times'. The aim is to love the Lord thy God with all thy heart, thy soul, thy mind, and thy strength, and thy neighbour as thyself.

"There were many problems in adapting, but I've loved working on it and I have seen many wonderful answers to prayer. Thank you for praying for this ol' bird. The Club is to be for both boys and girls, but not mixed. The material has not yet gone to the printers, as it seems necessary to wait for a while, but He is faithful. Believe that we'll be able to launch our first meeting in December, the Lord willing. Please pray that God will call forth Thai men and women for this work.

"Well, you guys, I didn't mean to go into these details, but I do love talking to you, and although this is a carbon, it's going to 'friends that are gold'. What a glorious day it will be when we all meet together at our Lord's feet where we shall worship and adore Him whom we love and serve – O glorious hope! Until then shall we continue to pray for one another? Although absent and far from one another, we are not able to forget His precious gift to us, 'Friendship', and all that He has taught us of Himself through one another. This comes with all my love for, to, and in Him who loved us and gave Himself for us. How can we do less?"

It was her last letter.

"I Have Finished My Course"

A FEW weeks after this triumphant letter had been mailed, Joan began to feel unwell. But she was never one to pamper herself, and although she had been indisposed for several days, she went out one morning to mow the lawn. This was a strenuous task which none of the other missionaries, and not even the servant, relished.

When it was finished Joan came into the house completely exhausted, but defended herself by saying, "My old aunt used to say if you don't feel well, just go out and do some hard work to get it out of your system." This time it was poor advice. Joan was advised to go to the OMF hospital in Manorom, and there her illness was diagnosed as infectious hepatitis and she was ordered to bed for four to six weeks.

No one was particularly alarmed, for hepatitis is a fairly common disease in the Far East and many of the other missionaries had had it. Although it requires many months of rest, it is seldom fatal. The main concern of the nurses, several of whom were close friends of Joan's, was that it might be difficult to keep active Joan in bed that long.

They soon found, however, that this was no problem, for the patient became very weak, eating little and sleeping much of the time. Yet when awake, she was bright and cheerful.

One day early in November Joan asked Carol Kealey, an American nurse, to take some dictation. She told her to draw four torches in a little book and to add the following inscriptions:

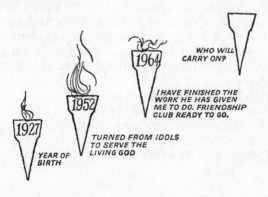

WHO WILL CARRY ON?

1964

I HAVE FINISHED THE WORK HE HAS GIVEN ME TO DO. FRIENDSHIP CLUB READY TO GO.

1952

TURNED FROM IDOLS TO SERVE THE LIVING GOD

1927

YEAR OF BIRTH

As the significance of the words came home to Carol, she said, "Joan, are you feeling that bad? Don't you remember the verse the Lord gave you the first morning you were sick?" (The verse had been, "This sickness is not unto death, but for the glory of God" John 11.4).

Joan's reply was, "But I have finished the work that He gave me to do," and with these words she told Carol to put the book away but to remember where it was. Neither referred to the matter again.

On November 7 Joan felt so much better that she even hoped to attend the coming annual field conference at Huahin, a seaside resort 300 miles to the south on the Gulf of Siam. She even planned some games for a party for Thai young people one evening, as the young doctor responsible was too busy to be present. But later she lapsed into drowsiness and could not go herself.

By November 12 most of the missionaries had left Manorom to attend the conference at Huahin and only a skeleton staff remained at the hospital. That very day Joan went into a coma, never to regain consciousness. The nurse said:

"I felt that Joanie left us on Thursday morning and we just took care of her house after that."

Telegrams telling of Joan's deteriorating condition reached the conference on successive days, and the ninety missionaries gathered prayed earnestly for her life. Cables also went across the ocean to Pioneer Girls' headquarters, from where an S.O.S. for prayer was sent to all board and staff members. Joan's life hung in the balance, but even as many prayed, some sensed that God was saying gently but firmly:

"It's all settled. I'm going to take her."

Several of her friends left the conference to be with Joan at this critical time. Dorothy Mainhood, sitting at the bedside, wrote to Joan's brother:

"I never dared let myself think that this hepatitis could

mean the end of her life on earth, until I heard how she herself had said that she had finished the work God had given her to do. Friendship Club hasn't been launched yet – I keep wanting to argue with her and call her back – but . . . "

The next day Dorothy continued:

"You will know by now that Joanie went to be with Jesus this morning. It was 4.15 a.m. Nurses consider this the darkest hour of the night. But just before she went, Carol and I prayed together and asked God to banish the darkness and all its powers. It was just ten minutes later when she quietly breathed her last and I knew she had left us to be with the One she loved more . . . I am so comforted to know she is in God's house where there is nothing but love. And one day she will welcome us there."

Carol Kealey wrote: "Because of the Lord's promise to her we prayed that she would be healed. However, I believe He has taught us that indeed this sickness was not unto death but unto eternal life and for the glory of God in many lives. I can't think of anyone who would rather go to be with Jesus than Joan."

Joan was buried in the only Protestant cemetery in Bangkok, located on the bank of the river Chao Phraya up which Joan had sailed for the first time in 1957, seven years before. Mrs. Cyril Faulkner wrote of the funeral:

"Many friends were present, for she had endeared herself to a wide circle, both Thai and missionaries. I went out in the morning to help arrange the flowers around the teak casket. The Thai church loaned us pots of green palms, and roses were tastefully arranged in the foreground. Her Thai name, Kulab, means 'Rose' and her life was as lovely and fragrant as one. The verse she used so much 'Called to reveal Christ in me' was real and her words were underscored by her love for Him and others. She loved much and prayed for so many."

Back in the homeland, Louise Troup, director of Pioneer Girls, broke the news to staff members: "Even as we shed tears over the loss of a dear friend, let us consider the glory she is experiencing beholding the face of Christ. How much she loved Him!"

But why should God take her so soon? She was still young and full of life. Humanly speaking, her work in Thailand was just beginning. Friendship Club was ready to be launched. Who can explain the mind of the Lord or understand His ways? We only know He makes no mistakes. Joan had fulfilled her part in Friendship Club and God must have others in mind to carry it on.

Joan Killilea's work on earth is done, but her life will long continue to speak. A missionary in North Thailand, Lyman Reed, who had known Joan since college days, expressed what many feel when they think of Joan.

"To us she was a trophy of God's matchless grace, genuine to the core, with an abounding love to her Lord; she loved and enjoyed life; her radiant personality never ceased to infect others. My wife and I think of her as a fragrant flower and the beauty of her selfless life and Spirit-taught virtues will linger long in our memories. Something of the life of Christ was revealed to us in her and we were blessed, giving thanks to Him for causing the pathways of our lives to cross."

Joan Killilea is a perfect example of God's handiwork. How could a child so deprived of love and security grow into a woman whose life radiated love in such measure? Who would have dreamed that this unpromising, lonely high school girl would some day influence so many lives? How could a life of restless, aimless drifting and adventure-seeking take on such deep meaning and steadfast purpose?

There is but one answer – GOD.